Comments on other *Amazing Stories* from readers & reviewers

"*You might call them the non-fiction response to Harlequin romances: easy to consume and potentially addictive.*"
Robert Martin, *The Chronicle Herald*

"*Tightly written volumes filled with lots of wit and humour about famous and infamous Canadians.*"
Eric Shackleton, *The Globe and Mail*

"*This is popular history as it should be... For this price, buy two and give one to a friend.*"
Terry Cook, a reader from Ottawa, on **Rebel Women**

"*Stories are rich in description, and bristle with a clever, stylish realness.*"
Mark Weber, *Central Alberta Advisor,* on **Ghost Town Stories II**

"*The resulting book is one readers will want to share with all the women in their lives.*"
Lynn Martel, *Rocky Mountain Outlook,* on **Women Explorers**

"[The books are] *long on plot and character and short on the sort of technical analysis that can be dreary for all but the most committed academic.*"
Robert Martin, *The Chronicle Herald*

"*A compelling read. Bertin...has selected only the most intriguing tales, which she narrates with a wealth of detail.*"
Joyce Glasner, *New Brunswick Reader,* on **Strange Events**

"*The heightened sense of drama and intrigue, combined with a good dose of human interest is what sets* Amazing Stories *apart.*"
Pamela Klaffke, *Calgary Herald*

CANADA'S PEACEKEEPERS

AMAZING STORIES®

CANADA'S PEACEKEEPERS

Protecting Human Rights
Around the World

MILITARY/HUMAN INTEREST

by Sheila Enslev Johnston

PUBLISHED BY ALTITUDE PUBLISHING CANADA LTD.
1500 Railway Avenue, Canmore, Alberta T1W 1P6
www.altitudepublishing.com
www.amazingstories.ca
1-800-957-6888

Extreme care has been taken to ensure that all information presented in
this book is accurate and up to date. Neither the author nor the
publisher can be held responsible for any errors.

Publisher	Stephen Hutchings
Associate Publisher	Kara Turner
Editor	Deborah Lawson
Layout and cover design	Bryan Pezzi

We acknowledge the financial support of the Government
of Canada through the Book Publishing Industry Development
Program (BPIDP) for our publishing activities.

Altitude GreenTree Program
Altitude Publishing will plant twice as many trees as were used
in the manufacturing of this product.

Library and Archives Canada Cataloguing in Publication

Enslev Johnston, Sheila
   Canada's peacekeepers / Sheila Enslev Johnston.

(Amazing stories)
Includes bibliographical references.
ISBN 1-55439-063-X

   1. Peacekeeping forces--Canada. 2. Peacekeeping forces--
Canada--History. I. Title. II. Series: Amazing stories (Canmore, Alta.)

JZ6377.C3E58 2005   355.3'57'0971   C2005-906647-4

Printed and bound in Canada by Friesens
2 4 6 8 9 7 5 3 1

To my Aunt, Karen Mitchell
For always believing ...

Contents

Lt. Gen. The Honourable Roméo Dallaire (Ret'd), Senator

Foreword

The author has been able to capture the essence of the complexities of modern soldiering, where there is no clear line between "the good guys" and "the bad guys," in recounting the personal stories of Canadian soldiers on these pages. It was and is an honour to serve one's country on missions whose aims are to bring peace and security to those whose lives are in peril. The defence and promotion of human rights can only make the world a better place.

Roméo A. Dallaire, Lieutenant General (Retired)

Prologue
Incident on Virunga Mountain

"Confirmed. They're all dead except for one little girl. Over."
The radio crackled with the poor reception, but the meaning was all too clear.

At his desk in Rwanda's capital city of Kigali, Brigadier General Roméo A. Dallaire looked up at the calendar: November 24, 1993. Dallaire hung his head. What he had feared would happen was beginning.

"Any indication of who committed these acts? Over."

Out at the scene of the incident, Virunga Mountain in the northwest corner of Rwanda, Canadian peacekeeper Major Brent Beardsley swallowed hard to clear his voice before transmitting a reply. "There were five little girls and one boy. They couldn't have been any older than nine or ten. It's clear that they were all strangled. One of the little girls is still alive, but she's in very rough shape. I'm afraid we won't get any information out of her. Over"

Dallaire shook his head. It was the same thing they seemed to meet at every turn — the sense of a mysterious faction spreading hatred and destabilizing the peace process. "Is there any evidence there at all? Over."

Major Beardsley hesitated, the radio microphone in his hand. Turning his head, he surveyed the scene again.

"There is something, but it doesn't make any sense. We found a glove in the same colour pattern as what the rebel army is wearing, but that just doesn't fit the scenario. This doesn't look like the sort of attack the rebels mount. Over."

Neither Canadian believed the rebels would have strangled young children to death, for no apparent reason, out in the middle of nowhere. They may have been ruthless, but they were smart. They had nothing to gain from an attack like this. Besides, they weren't likely to have been sloppy enough to leave evidence behind.

Dallaire shook his head again before giving his final instructions. "Understood. All right, collect all the evidence you can. Maybe the little girl who survived will be able to tell us something. Over."

"Roger," Beardsley replied. "There is one other thing. I don't trust the translator we have here. I told him to ask the locals who they thought could have committed such a crime. But I think he was coaching them. Over."

"Coaching them to say what? Over."

"Coaching them to say the rebels did it. Over."

Both men knew that the government blamed everything on the rebels.

Dallaire let out his breath in frustration.

Prologue

"All right. Get off that mountain before it gets dark. Over."

"Roger. Out." Beardsley signed off. Looking at the row of dead children in front of him, he sighed deeply. Just weeks earlier, back in Canada, he had seen his third child born. Now here he was, thousands of kilometres away from Canada, mourning these children he had never known.

"This is going to be bad," he said to himself. "Very bad."

Chapter 1
The Balkans — The Road to Sarajevo

Trucks and buses blocked the route. As the sun came up on the scene, Canadian soldiers could see the motley assortment of vehicles, all parked together to block the way across the narrow old bridge and through several tunnels.

Central Bosnia is a land of steep forested hills and small valleys cut with rapid rivers and streams. The little town of Jajce lay in one of those valleys, straddling the river Vrbas. Lieutenant Colonel Jones and the soldiers of his battalion would have to pass through Jajce to reach Sarajevo.

"Have the armoured engineer vehicles come forward to remove the blocking vehicles, and get the men to take up firing positions to protect the engineers," Jones ordered.

"We have to get through. Push them out of the way with the armoured engineer vehicles if you have to."

It was June 30, 1992, and they were on their way to Sarajevo to secure the airport for the United Nations (UN) forces there. Brigadier General Lewis Mackenzie had personally picked Jones's battalion for the crucial mission to secure the airport. Jones wanted to reach their objective by the next day, Canada Day.

The battalion of the Royal 22nd Regiment, famously known as the "Van Doos" (from *vingt-deux,* the French word for 22), had arrived in the former Yugoslavia in April of 1992. They were part of the initial contingent of the United Nations Protection Force, or UNPROFOR. UNPROFOR was the first of the new wave of UN peacekeeping missions that followed hard on the heels of the Cold War's end in the 1990s. The battalion was sent to the former Yugoslavia in 1992 when the communist state of Yugoslavia dissolved into civil war.

The Van Doos were originally sent to Croatia, where the Yugoslav civil war was then raging most fiercely. In Croatia, which had been a republic within the old state of Yugoslavia, fighting had broken out in the area where ethnic Serbs were concentrated. This area was known as the Krajina (pronounced "Kry-heen-ah"), and for centuries had been the home of ethnic Serbs who were citizens of the former Yugoslavia. In the maelstrom of this latest Yugoslav civil war, they had become a flashpoint of contention. After a ceasefire and a separation of the warring factions, these areas would be patrolled by UNPROFOR troops. It was hoped that the future of these disputed territories could then be negotiated peacefully.

While the combat troops were deployed in Croatia, it was decided that Sarajevo would be the ideal place for UNPROFOR's headquarters and rear area support. Because the conflict zones in Croatia lay in an arc shape around Bosnia, Sarajevo constituted a central location, providing almost equal road access to all four of the United Nations Protected Areas (UNPAs).

When UNPROFOR was first established, Bosnia was still peaceful, if somewhat uneasily so. A significant UNPROFOR presence in Sarajevo was likely to stabilize the tense situation there.

The leader chosen for this group of primarily logistic and administrative personnel was a previously obscure Canadian brigadier general by the name of Lewis MacKenzie.

When the fires of the Yugoslav civil war spread to Bosnia, MacKenzie realized he needed troops to secure the city's crucial airport, and that they couldn't wait for the UN to debate sending additional ones. The only way to get forces there quickly enough would be to move one of the units they already had in Croatia. MacKenzie had no doubt who he wanted for the job — the Van Doos.

But first the Van Doos had to get there. It was over 300 kilometres to Sarajevo from their camp at Daruvar. Poor quality roads crawled through the mountainous terrain typical of

Bosnia. But difficult as it sometimes was, driving would not be the greatest obstacle. Their route ran through the territory of all three of the country's ethnic factions. The Van Doos would have to pass through innumerable checkpoints and local skirmishes before reaching Sarajevo.

After hurriedly preparing themselves and their equipment, they formed into columns for the long move. The columns set out at midnight on June 29. The first hours of the trip passed smoothly enough, and after an uneventful refueling in Bosnian Serb controlled Banja Luka, they pushed on.

Their first major difficulty had come in Jajce, where Bosnian Croats had blocked the bridge and tunnels with vehicles to prevent the capture of the town by Bosnian Serbs. But Jones's gambit of seizing the vehicles and moving them out of the way worked, and the long Canadian column passed through without further incident. The Canadians even put the moved vehicles back in their original positions, once all their troops were through.

By the time they were out of Jajce, the sun was well up in the sky. In the mountainous central area of Bosnia, the journey became ever more tortuous. Vehicles — including trucks onto which huge sea containers had been lashed — ground their gears as they climbed narrow, winding roads higher and higher into the steep forested hills. Shortly before sundown they reached a high point just past the town of Donji Vakuf, and found themselves looking down upon a panoramic scene. The little village of Turbe, huddled into the valley, was the scene of active firing; they heard small-arms fire and saw occasional muzzle blasts from heavier weapons. Looking more closely, the Van Doos realized that figures of soldiers from the opposing sides were discernible along what could only be the front line between Bosnian Serbs and Bosnian Muslims. They even saw some Serbian tanks firing occasional shots into the Muslim-held town. Closer by, at Serbian mortar installations, soldiers were busy around their weapons, firing mortar bombs that arced up into the air with an audible *ca-chunk* before exploding on Muslim positions. This was the hottest zone they had encountered yet.

Suddenly, a car came careening up towards the Van Doo column. It screeched to a stop in front of Jones's Iltis jeep, blocking the road. The entire column ground to a halt. Jones examined the car for a moment before gesturing to his translator, Sergeant Vladislavjevich, a Canadian soldier of Yugoslav extraction who spoke Serbo-Croatian and went by the nickname of Vlad. The two Canadians climbed out of the Iltis and approached the car, wondering what was coming next.

Three men piled out of the car in a state of considerable agitation. The one who appeared to be the leader looked to be in his late forties. Greying, and dressed in an old and worn federal Yugoslav officer's uniform, the man was unshaven and disheveled. What worried Jones more was that the man was clearly drunk, always a danger sign. The two men behind him, disreputable looking civilians in ill-fitting, unkempt suits, appeared to be equally drunk.

Addressing his translator, Jones said, "Vlad, ask him what the problem is."

A brief exchange in Serbo-Croatian followed.

"He says we can't go through sir," the Canadian sergeant translated. "He says we have no business going to Sarajevo."

"Of course we have business going to Sarajevo — UN business. Tell him we have clearance from his own side's corps commander to pass through."

"Who are the other two men?" Jones asked, attempting a different tack.

"He says they're his political advisors," the translator explained. Jones couldn't help thinking this was a bad sign. Political hacks were more likely to be hard-line than were professional soldiers. Jones took note of the uniformed man's bleary eyes, wondering just how military he really was. *More of a local warlord than a real soldier,* Jones speculated silently.

Further exchanges produced increasing gesticulation by the Serb officer. The longer they talked, the more agitated and worked up he became.

Jones's Canadian troops had already been on the road for almost 20 hours. Deciding that he didn't want to risk a firefight between these three Serbs and his strung out and vulnerable column, Jones made a decision. With a final glare at the Bosnian Serb officer, he turned back to his column.

"All right," he said to his men. "We'll pull back, to just

this side of Jajce. Maybe by tomorrow they'll see sense, or will at least have heard from their commanders."

Bringing his attention back to the hostile officer, Jones eyed him squarely and said to Vlad, "Tell him we'll be back first thing tomorrow morning, and he'd better let us through then!" As Vlad translated this, Jones studied the Bosnian Serb's face, but it wasn't clear whether or not the man had processed the message.

Jones spun on his heel and stalked back to his jeep. The air filled with the revving sound of dozens of throaty diesel engines. Belching black bursts of smoke, they spun their tank tracks and peeled off, returning on the road over which they had just come.

Good soldiers can make themselves comfortable anywhere, and once the Van Doos reached the little Bosnian Croat-held town of Jajce and pulled off to the side of the road, it wasn't long before the men had camp stoves out and hot lunches on the go from their ration packs. Jones was preoccupied with more serious matters. After confirming that sentries were posted and that the troops were eating their first hot meal of the day, he grabbed a quick bite to eat, then called together an orders group with his key commanders and headquarters staff.

"We have to be ready to force our way through tomorrow morning," Jones said grimly. There was a pause while he let the implication of that sink in.

"First of all, I want to get hold of that Bosnian Serb

liaison officer. Get him down here, and let *him* tell those guys that we have their own corps commander's clearance to pass through."

"*Oui, mon colonel,*" the operations officer said. "I'll get right on that."

"Secondly," Jones continued, turning to Major Matern, the commander of C Company of the Van Doo battalion, "I want to move early tomorrow morning. H-hour will be 0500." Jones then laid out the details of his plan.

The next morning, near the place where they'd encountered the three men on the previous day, Jones and his men came upon a checkpoint. It was just a small log with concertina barbed wire attached, thrown across the road. But it was enough to block their way. Once again the column shuddered to a standstill. Beside the road was a small wooden cabin surrounded by the usual collection of ragged looking, lounging soldiers. As the Canadians pulled up the guards rose to their feet, unslinging their weapons.

Jones wasted no time jumping out of his jeep and stalking up to the cluster of Bosnian Serbs. Thankfully, he noted no sign that they were drinking anything stronger than coffee. In a loud voice, he demanded to see their commanding officer.

A man who appeared to be the roadblock commander came forward, as unshaven and scruffy looking as the rest, but sober.

"Good morning," Jones said firmly. "I am back."

Sergeant Vlad translated.

The man eyed Jones up and down, and then said something quickly.

"He says he has no authorization to let you through," Vlad explained.

"What does he mean, no authorization! I told them, we have the agreement of their corps commander!" Jones waved back towards the jeep. "Get that LO up here!" he shouted, referring to the Serbian liaison officer they had picked up the previous evening near Jajce.

The LO appeared and launched into a rapid discussion with the soldier at the roadblock. It wasn't necessary to have a translation to understand how the conversation was proceeding. The volume went up. Hand gestures became increasingly aggressive.

"He repeats himself," Sergeant Vlad said under his breath to Jones. "'No pass!' The LO is explaining that he represents their own corps commander, but it's not making any difference with this bunch."

Jones snorted. They'd already learned that command authority often meant very little amongst warring Balkan factions. This was just one more local warlord not under anyone's real control.

Suddenly Vlad called out "Sir! He's calling for reinforcements!"

Jones glared at the officer in charge. The Serbian soldier stared back stonily.

"Tell the roadblock commander," said Jones, between gritted teeth, "that if anyone else comes near the roadblock we will open fire without further warning."

Jones knew this was a bit of a bluff, but he was hoping the roadblock commander wouldn't realize that. He stalked back to his men, who were waiting patiently behind him, weapons at the ready.

The LO launched into another round of excited Serbo-Croatian with the checkpoint soldiers. After a tense few minutes, word came back from the increasingly nervous Serbs at the roadside.

"They say they've cancelled their call for reinforcements," Vlad translated. "They say their commander is coming back and wants to speak with us at the cabin."

A half hour of strained waiting later, the Bosnian Serb commander who had detained them the previous day pulled up in the same car. He was still stubble cheeked and scruffy looking, but to Jones's relief he was sober. After a preemptory nod, he headed to the small cabin with a civilian, who was to serve as his translator. Jones prepared to follow with Sergeant Vlad.

Realizing this was his chance to talk with the Serb commander one-on-one, he decided to leave the liaison officer out of it. Urgently, Jones turned to his own men and said, under his breath, "Deploy the snipers. Be ready to take control of the roadblock and block the road. Nobody gets through."

Behind him, the soldier in the first vehicle's machine gun hatch spun around a little in his turret. He cocked the machine gun, loudly and decisively. From inside the vehicle, Jones heard the squawk of the radio as the orders were being passed back.

Satisfied with his preparations, Jones headed over to the little cabin. He found the Bosnian Serb officer sitting on a bench outside the hut, with a stony expression on his face. Before Jones could say anything, the man spat out some words in Serbo-Croatian and gestured back up the road, in the direction of Jajce.

"He says we should turn around and go back again, like we did yesterday," Sergeant Vlad reported.

"I'm afraid I can't do that," Jones replied. "I have orders to move to Sarajevo. And I have your own corps commander's permission to pass through."

After another exchange Vlad reported, "He says you shouldn't be so concerned about official authorizations, or about going to Sarajevo. He says we don't have any business going there, and we should go back."

After a few more minutes of fruitless arguing back and forth through the translators, Jones finally snapped. "All right then, follow me! We'll see your own liaison officer!"

They strode over to confer with the Serbian liaison officer. The LO repeated once again that the regional corps commander had pledged his word that the Canadian column would be allowed to pass. He seemed vaguely embarrassed that he could not secure the cooperation of a fellow Bosnian Serb.

By this time, however, it was clear to the checkpoint personnel that something was afoot.

Jones's men now blocked the road. His snipers had taken up positions on the mountain slopes, covering the checkpoint and the cabin area. Orders were issued for the capture of the roadblock. Van Doos took up firing positions in close proximity to the increasingly nervous Bosnian Serb soldiers. And behind them, Captain Bérubé of the battalion's reconnaissance platoon led his men forward on foot, in preparation for seizing the roadblock position.

Faced with the deploying Van Doos, the checkpoint guards grew nervous, fingering their weapons. Their commander stopped arguing with the liaison officer, staring at the Canadians with venom in his eyes. Suddenly, Major Matern's voice rang out in French with fire control orders. Jones wasn't sure the guards understood the words, but they certainly seemed to get the gist of it as they heard and saw the Canadian soldiers cocking their weapons.

Apprehensively, the Serb commander licked his lips and then nodded towards a couple of thuggish civilian men who had arrived with him in the car. These were not the political advisors with whom he'd arrived yesterday. *They look like bodyguards*, Jones thought. It seemed as though the Bosnian Serb had arrived expecting the negotiations to fail.

As the two dangerous looking men closed up to their

commander, two of Jones's men closed up to their own leader. Captain Belisle, Lieutenant Colonel Jones's battle captain, and Master Corporal Cyr came around to the front of the cabin as well. They all felt the tension ratcheting up. Slung over Master Corporal Cyr's shoulder, ready for firing, hung an open M-72, a small bazooka-like anti-tank rocket that comes packed in a firing tube, about a metre long.

As Jones's men approached the tense negotiators, conversation stopped abruptly. All eyes swung towards the two young Canadian soldiers. Behind them, the Serbs could clearly see that the men of C Company were ready for action.

Jones held his breath, inwardly praying that no shooting would break out. With so many troops packed together around the roadblock, a firefight was bound to be murderous.

The standoff continued for what seemed, to Jones, ages. In reality, it must have been only a minute or two. Finally, the Bosnian Serb officer broke off eye contact and grunted something to his men. His translator said, "My commander asks that you let him confer with our corps headquarters. Maybe he will be able to bring you information on our mine fields."

Jones let out his breath with relief.

The Bosnian Serb commander then changed his demeanor completely, favouring them with a huge, insincere looking smile. Jones managed a thin smile in return and said to the translator, "Please thank your commander for me, and assure him that we would be most pleased to have him consult with your corps commander."

A short time later the roadblock was pulled aside and the Canadians moved through. Jones, however, could not shake a strong sense of distrust about the whole encounter. Once the Van Doos passed out of sight of the checkpoint, Jones changed their intended route, taking the column up a side road and through the hills towards Sarajevo. The alternative route was even more convoluted than the main road. With their big trucks full of equipment and supplies, progress was much slower than he had planned. The Van Doos would not make it to Sarajevo on Canada Day.

Just before 11 a.m. on July 2, the convoy reached the airport. Everything was ready. UN personnel waited for them at the chain-link gate, where the road led onto the scarred and damaged airport property. Guides directed the line of Canadian armoured vehicles to their proper positions, smoothly and professionally. While Jones watched with satisfaction from the armoured personnel carrier (APC) that served as his tactical command post, a white, armoured UN vehicle from the French contingent rushed up and careened to a halt. The energetic figure of Brigadier General Lewis MacKenzie bounded out and approached Jones, who pulled off his radio headset and descended to meet him. There were no salutes, due to the ever-present threat from snipers who particularly targeted officers. Instead, MacKenzie laconically asked, "Good trip?"

Equally dryly, Jones replied, "Not bad. Sorry I wasn't here for Canada Day."

MacKenzie grinned and stuck out his hand for a congratulatory shake. "Thank God you're here. I was worried that one of the factions wouldn't let you through, or would fire on you from the hills."

But the Van Doos had made it. Made it through the lines of multiple warring factions, stared down the antagonistic Bosnian Serbs, and forced their way into the besieged capital. They were the first regular United Nations unit to arrive in Sarajevo. Outnumbered though they were, they went on to secure the airport for the beleaguered UN forces.

The era of post-Cold War peacekeeping had begun.

Chapter 2
UNPROFOR —
The Medak Pocket

*here would the Croatians attack?* Major Dan Drew pondered silently, as he scanned the countryside from his small Iltis jeep. Newly promoted, and newly arrived in the Balkans, the Major finally found himself doing "for real" what he had only done during training, over and over again throughout his career. On this cool, damp May morning, conducting reconnaissance in Croatia's Sector West, he was seeking a full defensive position for his company of just over 100 soldiers.

Clearly, Major Drew realized, any Croatian attack would come along the main road that ran through the valley and the town of Pakrac. From his slightly elevated position he could see the road's long grey line snaking through the gently rolling countryside. Looking back and forth from his map to the actual view, he pondered potential targets, fields of fire, and areas of cover.

Here, he thought decisively. *This is the spot.* His company would dig their trenches and fire positions on the rise where he stood.

Once again he poured over the details of his map. Had he missed anything? Was there anything else he should allow for? His commanding officer, Lieutenant Colonel Jim Calvin, had impressed upon him the importance of this mission. The Croatians were becoming increasingly bold in challenging the cease-fire. UN higher command was worried that they would attempt a probe into Sector West, the most vulnerable of the UNPAs. It had been decided to prepare for the worst and, at the same time, send a clear message to the Croatian belligerents. As a result, the 800-plus soldiers of the 2nd Battalion, the Princess Patricia's Canadian Light Infantry (famously known as the PPCLI, "the Patricia's," or "Princess Pat's") were preparing fully combat-ready, defensive positions, carefully sited to block any attempt to drive into Sector West.

So it was that Major Drew, in command of D Company–PPCLI, found himself surveying the countryside and preparing orders for his men. Soon they would arrive in their M-113 armoured personnel carriers to begin digging defensive positions at the site he had chosen.

As it turned out, D Company never did face a Croatian attack along that route. Perhaps deterred by the robust defensive positions the PPCLI had created in the area, the

Croatians were conspicuously absent from Sector West during 2 PPCLI's Balkan tour, that spring and summer of 1993. Instead, the Canadians' mission settled into a routine of patrolling the area, monitoring cease-fire violations, and conducting cordon and search operations to find hidden weapons and other violations. By June, the Patricia's were confident they had gained control of the area and were on top of their game. Larger events, however, were about to draw them into Canada's fiercest fire-fight since the 1974 Turkish invasion of Cyprus, perhaps even since the Korean war.

The previous summer, Lieutenant Colonel Michel Jones and his battalion of Van Doos had moved to Sarajevo to secure the airport there. Surrounded on three sides, Sector West was considered the most vulnerable of Croatia's UNPAs. To back-fill the hole the Van Doos' departure had left in Sector West, other infantry battalions, in sequential rotation, had protected the area. Now it was 2 PPCLI's turn at the Van Doos' old stomping ground.

But as it turned out, things were heating up more dangerously in Sector South, near the Dalmatian coast. As cease-fire violations increased, the UN high command feared the volatile Croatians were about to test the UN's resolve to maintain the agreed-upon cease-fire lines. UNPROFOR headquarters in Zagreb decided they needed their best troops in Sector South.

Accordingly, word came down to Lieutenant Colonel Calvin and his PPCLI battalion. They were to leave behind one company, along with a few other soldiers, to hold the Sector West positions, and redeploy the bulk of their unit to Sector South. After a few moves, the Patricia's eventually deployed in a long narrow valley near the small town of Medak. UNPROFOR then decided to move the entire Canadian battalion down to Sector South permanently. By early September, the entire battalion was established in the Medak area, the very spot where the Croatians had decided to probe Serb defences and UN resolve.

Croatian troops had pushed down the west side of the valley, capturing the small villages of Citlik and Licki Citlik, and had almost reached the town of Medak itself. In response, Krajina Serb reinforcements had streamed into the area and dug in. It was clear to all of the Patricia's just how serious the circumstances were. Now was the time to seize control of the situation and force the two sides apart, and the reunited 2 PPCLI was ready for the challenge.

Canadian positions had been subjected to occasional artillery fire for several days, sometimes clearly deliberately. On the afternoon of September 14, Lieutenant Colonel Calvin assembled all headquarters staff and key PPCLI officers, and held his orders group. Later, they would relay the orders down the chain of command until everyone in the battalion knew exactly what they would have to do the next day.

The plan was for the Canadian battalion to advance into the valley that the Croatians had captured, secure the area, and oversee a withdrawal — by both sides — back to previous cease-fire lines. A political agreement for this had just been struck at the highest levels in Zagreb.

But had local Croatian forces been informed of the latest political deal? Nobody knew for certain. Nevertheless, it was absolutely imperative that PPCLI troops go ahead with the operation to separate the two sides. If they did not, the UN force might well lose all credibility. Even more ominous was the possibility they would lose control of the whole situation. The stakes could not have been higher.

The only good news was that, because of the importance of the situation, two companies of French mechanized infantry had been brought in specifically for this operation, to reinforce the Patricia's . The French companies were much larger than Canadian ones, numbering about 200 soldiers each. And they came with their APCs, on each of which were mounted powerful, 20-millimetre cannons.

Grimly, Calvin oversaw the finishing touches to the operations order for the next day's undertaking. One of the two French companies would lead off the advance on the right; C Company of the Patricia's would take the left. Behind each of these leading companies would be another company, held ready to follow when ordered forward, to ensure the Croatians withdrew to the agreed-upon cease-fire line. Dan Drew and the men of D Company would perform this role on the left, while the second French company took the right. Lieutenant Colonel Calvin would be there to oversee the start of the advance.

H-hour was set for noon. While Calvin and his staff burned the midnight oil, pouring over every detail of the plan again and again, the troops passed an uneasy night in their positions. The occasional sounds of distant shooting and artillery fire only increased their disquiet.

Shortly before the noon H-Hour, all the troops were assembled just in front of the village of Medak, ready to move out in their armoured personnel carriers. Then, unexpectedly, General Cot of the French army (who was the UN commander in Croatia) arrived in a helicopter. As soon as it landed, Cot bounded out, crouching beneath the whirling helicopter blades, and strode directly to a slightly startled Lieutenant Colonel Calvin. The French general wanted to review the situation personally before any troops went in. Courteously, Calvin escorted him around, let him speak to the French company commanders, and explained the PPCLI plan. Satisfied, Cot gave his okay for the operation to proceed and disappeared, as swiftly as he had appeared, into the air.

By the time General Cot departed it was past noon. Calvin quickly re-set the time for the advance to 1400 hours (2 p.m.). As the new H-Hour approached, C Company's 15 boxy M-113 armoured personnel carriers revved their diesel engines, pulling forward from the line of departure. Cautiously, in column formation, they trundled off along the narrow dirt track towards the valley where the fighting had been, each one throwing up a dust cloud in the hot summer sunshine.

The instant they came within sight of the Croatian army's positions, the four APCs of the lead platoon came under attack. Rifle shots and sporadic bursts of machine gun fire raked the vehicles. Instinctively, the men ducked inside. Crew commanders barked orders into their intercoms; drivers gunned their vehicles towards the slight cover of the first tree line. The platoon commander, 26-year-old Lieutenant Tyrone Green, pulled up to survey the countryside. From the top hatch of his APC, he swept his binoculars back and forth. Although it was hard to see anything definite, the assault was clearly coming from forward positions of the Croatian defenses, which were scattered across the valley floor before them.

The radio crackled with questions from his superiors. Lieutenant Green reported that the attack had been carried out with small-arms fire only. Quick consultations circulated up and down the battalion's chain of command. Calvin wanted his vanguard force to push on. Perhaps the Croatians had mistaken the Canadians for a Serb counter-attack. Surely, once the Croatians saw clearly who it was, they would realize the truth — that was this was a Canadian UN force, arriving to enforce the recent agreement.

An order squawked over the radios. To make their identity as clear as possible, all APCs were instructed to fly UN flags. Hastily, soldiers scrambled out the hatches and hung the flags from the radio antennas. When they were done, the flagged, UN-white APCs pulled out once again.

Almost immediately they were faced with a hail of fire.

This time, the small-arms rounds ricocheting off the sides of their vehicles were joined by heavy machine gun fire. Suddenly, the men spotted the smoke trails of rocket-pro- pelled grenades, or RPGs. Designed by the Russians, and common weapons throughout the former Yugoslavia, RPGs are the modern descendents of World War II "bazooka" anti- tank rockets. Their small warheads exploded on contact and could easily "brew-up" the comparatively thinly armoured M-113s, disintegrating the metal.

Yelling warnings into their radio headsets, platoon drivers crashed their vehicles into the safety of the ditches. Behind them, the rest of the company went to ground in whatever cover they could find. Clearly, the Croats had no intention of honouring the agreement and letting the Canadians proceed.

As the attack continued, the Patricia's returned fire, shooting directly at the forward-most Croatian positions. Crewmen fired the big .50 calibre heavy machine guns mount- ed on their APCs, while others joined in with light machine guns or personal weapons. Soon both the Canadians and the Croatians were immobile, pinned down in the firefight.

Calvin ordered his men to hold in place and immediately sought a meeting with the senior local Croatian commander. That evening, Calvin, the battalion's Regimental Sergeant Major, and Major Drew, passed through the Croatian lines on foot. An escort drove them to the Croatian Area Headquarters in the nearby town of Gospic, where they met with General

Ademi, the local Croatian Sector Commander. Meanwhile, Canadian troops remained in their tactical positions, exchanging occasional bursts of gunfire with the Croatians.

A tense night passed. The two Canadian officers eventually obtained Ademi's grudging consent to allow the UN force to implement the peace agreement the next day. It was decided that C Company would remain where they were. The approximately 100 men of Major Drew's D Company would move forward, passing through C Company's positions, along what now constituted a front-line. D Company would then advance into the valley to secure the area specified in the cease-fire and withdrawal agreement.

September 16 dawned sunny and warm, a gorgeous late-summer morning. But the men of 2 PPCLI were too haggard and bleary eyed to appreciate it. C Company had spent most of the night on alert, caught up in occasional firefights. Under cover of darkness, D Company had moved forward to the planned crossing site. No one had slept.

Once again, H-Hour was delayed while efforts were made to ensure that the Croatians would comply with the agreement. At noon, D Company's armoured personnel carriers moved off, heading down the dirt road towards the agreed-upon crossing point. Calvin was there to oversee personally. But so was a gaggle of news reporters and TV cameramen who had appeared that morning. It made for a disturbingly vulnerable convoy as D Company moved towards the Croatian front line.

But their way wasn't yet free of complications. Although the troops encountered no further gunfire, Croatian sentries adamantly refused to let the Canadians pass. D Company's APCs, caught in convoy formation, began to bunch up along the little road. Still, the Croatian soldiers refused to budge.

Ominously, soldiers from one of their "Guards Brigades" began to deploy into fire positions, overlooking the column of Canadian APCs. Weapons were cocked on both sides. The Canadians stood their ground grimly, staring into the mouths of the Croatian guns and demanding to be let through. It was a Mexican standoff.

Calvin made his way to the front of the column. The Croatian officer at the crossing point looked nervous, but remained adamant. Thinking fast, Calvin made a snap decision. "Get those reporters up here!" he barked to his men.

Standing with his back to the Croatians, so the TV cameras had a clear view of the roadblock and the valley beyond, Lieutenant Colonel Calvin held an impromptu press conference, directly under the Croatians' levelled guns.

"As you can see," Calvin explained, "the Croatian military is not honouring their own agreement to allow the UN in to re-establish cease-fire lines. Behind me you see the Croatian roadblock. In the distance, you see smoke rising at the horizon. We might wonder why the Croatians will not allow us in to see what is causing that smoke."

It was a thinly veiled reference to ethnic cleansing.

When the Croatians saw how the situation would appear

Dugout in the Medak pocket

in the international media, they backed down and allowed D Company to go through. APCs trundled past the Croatian checkpoint and spread out across the valley floor. Slowly and grudgingly, the Croatian soldiers picked up and withdrew, returning to the cease-fire line.

With the tactical situation secured, the Canadians could turn their attention to the situation in the Medak pocket area. It was soon devastatingly apparent what had caused the smoke they had spotted from the roadblock. Every building in the area had been burned out.

Subsequent PPCLI investigations determined that large supplies of firewood had been brought in to start the fires, thus ensuring total destruction. To maximize the obliteration, the Croatians had rigged all large buildings with military explosives, blowing them up before they lit the fires.

Scattered around all of the buildings in the pocket, the Patricia's found hundreds of pairs of discarded surgical gloves. At first they found this odd, but eventually they were stunned to realize that these gloves had been used in a horrible crime. The only explanation that made any sense was that they had been used to handle large numbers of bodies.

Sixteen actual bodies were found in the wreckage, most of them badly burned. The bodies of two young women, estimated to have been between the ages of 15 and 25, were found in the basement of one burned out house, trapped in the remains of a small room that had a barred door. They had been shot, soaked in gasoline, and then burned. When the Canadians found them, the bodies were still so hot that they had to be doused with water, to cool them sufficiently so that the body bags would not melt. In another case, the body of an elderly woman, estimated to have been 70 to 80 years old, was found in a field. She had been shot four times, once in the head from close range. Attempts had even been made to kill all the livestock in the area. It was the all-too-common Balkan pattern.

But this savagery gave every appearance of having been rushed. The PPCLI's persistence in forcing their way into the Medak pocket had probably cut short one of the region's ethnic cleansings.

Chapter 3
Horse Aid

Mile Komasovic waited by the stable door for a pause in the shelling, which had been fierce for hours. The once majestic stud farm lay in ruins. Carcasses dotted the field, with splotches of blood showing bright red against snowy white coats. Many horses, neighing and wheeling in panic, were caught in the outer corrals. The noise of the mortars had frightened them and they were clearly agitated.

Spring 1991. War had come to the Lipik stud farm, one of the breeding farms for the famous Lipizzaner stallions of Vienna. With his heart aching at the sight of the beautiful, almost irreplaceable brood mares lying lifeless in the field, Miles turned to the horses he could still help. Quietly, moving from stall to stall, he whispered soft words to the skittish animals.

Komasovic, the director of the farm, knew the importance of remaining calm. The horses would be able to sense his panic, and they needed to be calm if he was to have any chance of moving them in an orderly fashion. He had no idea who was doing the shelling. He was neither a political man nor a soldier. He was just a passionate horse man, and he'd devoted his life to the horses of Lipik.

Pushing his own feelings down deep, he took the first horse from her stall and led her off to what he hoped was the relative safety of the nearby tree line. After securing and briefly comforting the high-strung horse, he returned to the stalls for another one. By the time the day was over, Komasovic had saved more than 80 horses, leading them away during breaks in the shelling. Thirteen lay dead in the fields. Three were stolen from the forest while he made his trips back and forth. As night fell, Komasovic stood with the horses, weary of soul and utterly baffled. Didn't those soldiers up in the hills — whoever they were — know that these were the most famous horses in the world?

Since Roman times, what is now Croatia had been famous as an area for superior horse breeding. The Lipizzaner stallion, originally bred solely for Austria's Hapsburg monarchy, is one of the most exclusive horse breeds in the world. When the breed was first established, a network of breeding farms throughout the Hapsburg empire supported it. After that empire fell, they became even more famous as the "Lipizzaner stallions," the remarkable, all-white show horses who perform in Vienna and tour around the world.

Some of the Lipizzaners' most important breeding farms were in Croatia. And one branch of the Lipizzaners, the Tulipans, had been bred exclusively at a stud farm in Lipik, Croatia.

There, on the northern bank of the Sava River, over 30 Lipizzaner stallions had been killed when shelling destroyed the farm in October of 1991. For nearly two years after that, however, the whereabouts of the other 80 horses that had lived at the farm was a mystery. Where was the rest of the herd?

In April 1993, Lieutenant Colonel Calvin heard that the Mayor of Pakrac had sent a letter to the UN requesting help for the Lipizzaner stallions and brood mares at the famous local farm. Calvin wasn't sure if there was any truth to the rumour. And although he had been told of the farm's existence, no one seemed to know its location.

As far as the Canadians knew, the horses had all been killed during the early days of the civil war. And until he located the letter, Calvin didn't know if there was even anything the Canadians could do to help. Neither was there any official interest in such an endeavour.

Most Canadians know about the good deeds of UN peacekeepers in delivering humanitarian aid. But horse aid? Because of the war, people were suffering and dying, and the area was under what was supposed to be a strictly controlled

Captain (now Major) Steven Murray with Mr. Komasovic
and one of the Lipizzaner stallions that was saved.

embargo. Neither the UN nor Canada wanted to get involved in a wild goose chase for a bunch of animals.

But back home in Ontario, Jim Calvin and his father had trained and raced standard bred horses, so Calvin knew about the Lipizzaner breed and was interested enough in their whereabouts to assign one of his young officers to find out what had happened to them. But first the letter had to be found.

This was the mission Lieutenant Colonel Calvin gave to Captain Stephen Murray, a young reservist attached to the PPCLI in the spring of 1993. It was a special mission that would take him on a madcap chase through contested check-points and into the heart of Serbia itself.

Murray began by looking into the history of the herd. Local Croatian officials told him that the horses had, indeed, been killed in the last of the Serbian advances. All 100 horses were thought to have perished. The farm's director was also missing. This, however, was less surprising to Lipik's primarily Croatian populace. Komasovic was an ethnic Serb. Maybe he had killed all the horses just before he left. Wasn't it just the sort of thing, the local Croats hinted darkly, that a Serb would do to their famous horses?

Such suspicion between Balkan factions was all too familiar to the young Canadian captain. *Now*, he thought somewhat wryly, *they're dragging animals into their internecine disputes,*

As he learned more about the breed's history, Murray sadly discovered that they had been repeatedly affected by the events of the humans that surrounded them. In fact, Murray's assignment was strangely similar to one ordered by the famous American Lieutenant General George S. Patton 50 years earlier at the end of World War II, when the Lipizzaners in Vienna had been endangered by another one of their masters' wars. That time, the retreating German army had made off with the horses and Patton had ordered a mission to recover them.

Patton, an Olympic equestrian rider, was keenly concerned with the fate of the horses and personally organized protection for them throughout the rest of World War II. At the end of the war the brood mares were returned to their traditional breeding farms, one of which was the facility in Lipik, where they were seen as a proud symbol of Croatian heritage. This latter fact, of course, was why the Croats alleged the Serbs had killed all the animals. It was a way to strike symbolically at the Croatian nation. Such acts were all too common in the Balkan civil wars of the 1990s.

But Murray couldn't help thinking there was more to the story, and he persisted in his search. Eventually it led him to the small town of Daruvar, which was the Canadians' base camp in the area at the time. What he found there was, in fact, a note from the mayor of Pakrac to the UN, requesting veterinary and medical aid for the Lipizzaners.

Now Captain Murray was able to put all the clues together, and figure out what had happened. The horses were still alive — and they were in Serbia!

The director of stud operations, Mile Komasovic, had managed to smuggle the 80 or so horses out of Lipik during the 1991 fighting, and they were stabled at a makeshift farm near Belgrade.

However, the international embargo in place against Serbia included veterinary medical supplies. There were simply none to be had. The Lipizzaner herd was being overrun with equine influenza, and nothing could be done without outside help.

Murray reported these developments to Calvin. They still couldn't drum up any official interest in the issue.

Without hesitation, Lieutenant Colonel Calvin contacted a friend back home in Winnipeg, a veterinarian by the name of Dr. Patricia Haugh. Pat and Jim had known each other for years. She knew of Jim's love for horses and also knew he was busy commanding the Canadian battalion in the middle of a war zone. If he was asking for her help, she knew it must be an extraordinary situation.

Pat acted. She first contacted some large-animal veterinarians in Winnipeg. She was a feline veterinarian and hadn't had any medical interaction with horses for years. She asked her colleagues to help her make a list of all the medical supplies and other products a horse farm would need. Ointments, vitamins, shampoo, iodine, liniments, cough syrup, and vaccines were just some of the items identified. Pat then turned to veterinarian supply companies and asked them to donate items that might be shipped over. To her delight, box after box began pouring into her clinic; so many, in fact, that she had to begin storing them at her home as well.

When all the supplies had been collected, Canadian military personnel from the PPCLI's home base in Winnipeg came and packed the supplies. Particular care had to be taken with items such as vaccines, which had to be kept on ice. Air Canada donated the transportation and soldiers loaded the boxes onto the plane. The precious cargo was flown straight through to Air Canada's offices in Vienna, Austria, to await pick up by Captain Steve Murray.

Of course, nothing is ever easy in the life of a UN peacekeeper. Tasked with bringing the supplies back to Daruvar, Captain Murray and two drivers, Corporals Cramer and Ramsey, left the Canadian camp in a UN vehicle to drive to Vienna. At the border of the newly independent country of Slovenia, however, they were denied entry. Slovenia was the only one of the former Yugoslav republics that had been able to avoid being sucked into the civil wars; it was anxious to distance itself from the conflict and from UNPROFOR soldiers. Murray and his men would not be allowed through without high-level clearance. And since this was a private initiative, they had no such papers.

Feeling rather secretive, and after several abortive attempts to locate an unpoliced border crossing, Murray told his drivers to return to Daruvar. He would undertake the mission himself. Dressed in civilian clothing, Captain Murray drove to Zagreb and scrounged up a rental car — a decrepit red Volvo sedan. It was barely roadworthy, but it would allow Murray to forego the trappings of the UN and undertake the mission as a private citizen. This got him through the border and he drove straight to the Vienna airport.

But picking up the thousands of dollars worth of veterinary supplies wasn't straightforward either. Customs fees were payable! Murray crossed his fingers and signed back over to Air Canada the entire bill for customs fees. He "hoped no one would mind."

The next challenge was the sheer number and size of the packages — including one refrigerator-sized crate. Filling the car with the boxes and strapping the large "fridge" into the trunk (only until out of sight of the punctilious Austrian officials who had forbade him to break down the crate), Murray squeezed into the miniscule remaining space and took off into the gorgeous Austrian countryside. After breaking down the "fridge" and securing the contents inside the sedan, he hoped the worst was over. He was already running behind schedule, and he hadn't even gotten back into Croatia. He knew this was likely to cause problems, since the last thing a border guard was going to do was allow him to return with medical supplies for horses in Serbia. Sure enough, he was challenged at his first checkpoint.

At this point in the unrest in Croatia, a rather vibrant underground market was emerging. Murray knew that a bribe offered in the direction of the border guard would make for a much easier crossing. Unfortunately, all his money had gone towards paying for the trip — and he didn't think the Croatian guard would accept his American Express. So Murray fully expected to be pulled over.

What he wasn't prepared for was the stone-faced guard that approached his little red vehicle. Leaning into the car through the open window, the guard peered suspiciously at the boxes and boxes of medical supplies. He waved over another guard and instructed Captain Murray to exit the vehicle. Nervously, Murray got out of the car and stepped to one side. Both guards were now kneeling in the front seat, inspecting the various boxes and bottles. Since everything was written in English, the guards couldn't understand the labels.

They did understand, however, that these were medical supplies. Not only that, but because of the amount and rarity of these supplies in the theatre of conflict, they would fetch an extremely high price on the underground market. The guards looked at each other in mutual agreement — and Murray knew exactly what they were thinking. There was nothing to stop them from "confiscating" his valuable cargo and then turning around and selling it themselves.

This gave Captain Murray more than one reason for being extremely apprehensive. Not only would the horses fail to receive critical aid, but there was also the potential for real danger if the medicines were sold for human use. They were meant for horses, not people.

Murray stared coolly at the border guards, determined to keep his composure, and mentally prepared himself for the round of questioning he knew was about to take place. In broken English, the first guard asked him what the supplies were. Since they were obviously medical supplies, Murray knew he was being tested.

"I'm a doctor," he lied, crossing his fingers yet again. "I am delivering these medical supplies to the UN camp in Daruvar."

The border guard shuffled his feet, looked off into the distance for a moment, then turned again to Murray.

With a penetrating stare, he ordered, "Make papers."

When Murray hesitated, he repeated, emphatically, "Papers!"
The young Canadian knew what this meant, in spite of the
guard's limited English. He wanted to see the official authorization that allowed Murray to enter the country with medical
supplies. Murray checked his wallet and dug through his pock-
ets, pretending to search for the requested papers and thinking madly all the while about how to approach the situation.

Standing with the guards beside the little wooden hut,
Murray continued his pantomime. A long trail of cars waited
behind the overloaded red car, waiting their turn to cross the
border. Drivers, becoming impatient, began to lean hard on
their horns, obviously upset that he was taking so much time.

Murray slapped himself on the head, making the international sign of forgetfulness. "I just don't know what happened to them," he said politely. "I must have left them
somewhere." He gestured towards his overloaded little car.

Murray knew he was lying, and he knew that the guard
knew he was lying. *This is where the bribe request will come,*
Murray thought.

"Make papers." The guard said it once again. Murray
shook his head.

"I don't seem to be able to find them," he answered.

Slyly, the guard looked at his co-worker. "One hundred
deutschmarks, then."

*That bit of English was spoken as clearly as if it were his
native tongue.* It was obvious to Murray that the guard had
used that line before.

Murray might have been tempted to try and pay them off, but he didn't have any cash left. "No money," he answered, showing them his empty wallet. "I'm afraid I'm broke."

Behind him a crowd was gathering — irate vehicle owners whose journey was now being halted at the border. Murray suddenly realized he might be able to use this to his advantage.

"Sorry guys," he said. "No money and no papers. So what's next?"

The guards were visibly agitated at this point. They waved him over to the hut at the side of the road and told him to go inside. He would have to talk to the border commander.

This was exactly what Murray had been hoping for. Cooperatively, he pulled the little red car off to the side of the road and stopped it in front of the hut. Watching from the rear view mirror, he saw what he had expected to see. Cars descended on the border guards in a flurry of activity as the locals tried to get on their way. Both guards were soon preoccupied.

Murray immediately stole his chance. Calmly, without looking back, he floored the gas pedal and tore off as fast as the little red car could go. The border guards saw him but there was little they could do, since the road was now blocked with other people. Murray heard the tail end of a profanity blasting through the air, and he laughed in spite of himself. He might not have been James Bond, but he was doing pretty darn well just the same!

Horse Aid

The day progressed in glorious sunshine. Captain Murray sped back to PPCLI base camp in Daruvar to change into uniform, pick up official transport, and return his civilian "rental" to Zagreb. The next hurdle would be nailing down exact directions to the farm where the horses were being held. The PPCLI had been told that some of the horses were now extremely ill. It was now going to be a race against time.

Through Serbian authorities in Pakrac, Captain Murray made contact with an older Serbian man by the name of Mr. Golic. He would guide Murray to the actual farm. And since the Croatians were extremely unlikely to allow a load of medical supplies and a Serbian passenger to leave the country, Murray made arrangements to meet Golic at the Canadian embassy in Belgrade, the capital of Serbia. With the precious supplies loaded into a light truck and Murray in an Iltis jeep to lead the way, the little convoy set off to cross the battle lines in eastern Croatia.

As they had feared, the Croatians at the border checkpoint did not want to let a supply of medical aid go anywhere near Serbia. Indeed, the international community itself technically forbade this under the embargo. Murray wondered, *Surely this doesn't include horse aid, too?*

In any event, he produced a letter on UN stationary and handed it over to the Croatian border guards, who peered at it skeptically. It wasn't really a high-level official clearance but, of course, the Croat guards couldn't read it. And it did *look* official. After some quick talking by the young Canadian officer, the guards, with great reluctance, allowed the little convoy to cross into Serbia.

Without stopping, Murray and his team raced on to Belgrade where Canadian embassy staff under Sgt. Mudge agreed to house the vehicles in their garage overnight. There, as planned, they met up with Golic. And the next day, with no further hitches, they proceeded to the farm. Murray finally saw the beautiful animals he'd gone to such lengths to save.

Miles Komasovic, the stud director who had rescued the horses from the shelling in 1991, greeted them with heartfelt relief. He and his small staff quickly unloaded the convoy's precious contents and went to work immediately, administering medicines to the horses.

All the Lipizzaners survived. Due to the compassionate action of Canadian peacekeepers, who expanded their duties to help not just the people of a war-torn area, but some sick horses as well, a long line of equestrian tradition and history will continue.

Chapter 4
Somalia — Stabilization and School Building

On a cracked, old runway in Somalia, a camouflage-painted Canadian CC-130 Hercules transport aircraft touched down and taxied to the edge of the dusty little airfield. Its giant turboprops still spinning thunderously, the aircraft turned around and dropped its rear ramp. From the back, Airborne Regiment soldiers charged out, weapons at the ready, and threw themselves to the ground in fire positions around the aircraft.

The Canadians had arrived in Baledogle to help secure Somalia and make it safe for humanitarian relief.

But they were not greeted by hostile warlords or rioting crowds. Nor was the airstrip empty. American military and various aid agency personnel were sitting around the edge of the airfield, many relaxing on lawn chairs. They clapped and cheered at the Canadians' performance. Reporters covered the scene, including one from the CBC. In fact, CBC journalists later asked them to repeat their "assault" landing, so the camera crew could get better pictures.

Somewhat sheepishly, the Canadian soldiers obliged, picking themselves up from the dusty ground and trudging back into the aircraft's hot interior. The Canadian Airborne Regiment hadn't known what circumstances they were getting into, so they had arrived tactically, prepared for anything. Somewhat later, with unloading well underway and soldiers streaming on and off the aircraft, starting the work of setting up the Canadian contingent, it seemed a surreal beginning for the mission. Sergeant Scotty Collins, a wise old non-commissioned officer (NCO) from the Airborne Servicing Commando, and the oldest member of the Airborne on the mission, tartly observed, "I hope we don't have to do things twice the whole time we're here."

Baledogle was not the Canadian Airborne's ultimate Somalian destination. Baledogle is a small airfield just northwest of the Somalian capital of Mogadishu, and the place where the Airborne Battle Group first landed and organized itself to move on. They were headed for the town of Belet Huen, almost 300 kilometres due north of Mogadishu and close to the Ethiopian border.

By 1992 Somalia was the classic example of a "failed state." After years of civil war and drought the government had all but collapsed. Power had reverted to the traditional clans, or simply to mafia-like local warlords. A surreal "Mad Max" landscape emerged, in which so-called "technicals" — small pick-up trucks with heavy machine guns or other improvised weapons mounted on their backs — roamed the countryside, fighting over territory or what few resources remained.

The drought had struck hard and mass starvation was spinning out of control. With heart wrenching scenes being beamed out of the country by the world's media, the international community decided to do something.

Aid could be rushed in, but for it to get through and to be effective required at least some order on the ground, and protection for relief workers. Because the country lacked a functioning government, it had neither civil order nor protection for individuals. A recognized government did not even exist that could invite an international peacekeeping force to assist in establishing order. Consequently, the UN decided to do something more than issue press releases and send humanitarian aid in the vain hope that some of it would get through safely. In December 1992, the United Nations Security Council passed a resolution authorizing an international contingent to land in Somalia and establish some basic security.

The result of that resolution was The Unified Task Force (UNITAF), a force led by the United States to intervene forcefully in Somalia and re-establish order. While authorized by the UN, it was not run by the UN, but by a U.S.-led coalition. This contingent was not being sent to Somalia to monitor a cease-fire or implement a peace agreement. It was being sent in to re-establish order by force, and it was fully authorized to use force to do so. In the soldiers' vernacular, it was a "peace making" mission, rather than a "peacekeeping" mission.

Although widely misunderstood, the Canadian Airborne's mission was to form Canada's contribution to UNITAF, the peace enforcement mission of a multi-national coalition. Their intent was to seize control of the area by armed force.

Unfortunately for the Airborne soldiers, this significant decision had been made only at the last moment, causing confusion. The mission was reorganized and re-planned repeatedly. The final reorganization took place while the Canadian Airborne Regiment Battle Group was actually en route to Somalia. They only learned that they were going to Baledogle a few hours before their arrival, during a stopover in Djibouti, a French territory on the coast of the nearby Red Sea.

Confusion reigned. On the one hand, they had heard about the arrival of U.S. Marines on the beaches at Mogadishu, where their tactical landing was met by hundreds of reporters rather than armed clansmen or warlords. On the other hand, there had also been conflicting reports of firefights, both between UNITAF forces and warlords, and between the rival warlords themselves. The Canadian soldiers hadn't known what to expect when they ran down the ramp, so they had come prepared for the worst — which explained their surreal arrival scene, charging off the first Hercules to the applause of waiting U.S. personnel and aid workers.

It wasn't long before the Canadians were moving north to their final destination, Belet Huen. Once again, a CC-130 Hercules transport aircraft transported the troops to a small airfield with a dirt runway. Belet Huen, they found, was a parched and baked desert, populated by stick-thin Somalis. A fine reddish dust, inescapable, worked its way into every-thing, clogging equipment. The airfield was abandoned and surrounded by impoverished squatters, and the town they saw from the runway looked rundown and destitute. It was a wind-swept and desolate place. It was also overcrowded with people who had streamed in from the surrounding country-side, driven off by the chaotic factional strife.

Sweating in the burning heat of the sun, and weighed down by weapons, ammunition, radios, and backpacks full of equipment, the Airborne soldiers moved out from the Hercs and set off on foot for the area they had selected for their camp. They began the long, hot work of setting up their base and accomplishing their mission.

Patrols began immediately, with small groups of sol-diers going out on foot with rifles and radios, beginning to make their presence felt in the area and establish a rapport with the locals. At night, they could often see and hear weap-ons fire in the distance, sometimes red and sometimes green tracers dancing in the black African nights. Every morning, Somali locals would pass, going to the graveyard to bury the night's dead. It was hard to dig in the parched earth, and they covered the shallow graves with rocks to prevent them from being dug up by the many wild dogs.

But gradually, by dint of vigilance and hard work, the Airborne began to make a difference. Open fighting subsided in the area, and life began to return to the town. More traders and merchants opened, trade goods began to travel again, and the Airborne negotiated relationships with local clan leaderships.

But the Canadian Airborne Battle Group sought to win over their sector not just by bringing order and relief supplies, but by longer term efforts. They wanted to re-establish society as well — what the armed forces refers to as civil military operations or "CIMIC," and the public generally calls "hearts and minds" operations.

These efforts went beyond the official tasks UNITAF assigned to Canadians for their sector. Many were bottom-up initiatives from the troops themselves. For instance, the Canadian military engineers in Belet Huen took it upon themselves not just to keep the roadway communication lines as open as possible and Canadian facilities functioning, but also to begin rebuilding local facilities such as schools. In some cases this was done in the soldiers' spare time.

* * *

Captain Jeremy Mansfield stood rooted to the spot in astonishment. The cheerful young officer, known to everyone by his nickname of "Jo Jo," was the leader of 23rd Field Squadron, the troop of military engineers attached to the Airborne Battle Group. He and his men and women had spent an entire day, together with some local Somalis, laboriously erecting a temporary bridge over the Shabeli River, which ran through the centre of town. Built at the site where the main road crossed the river, it was part of their effort to rebuild Somalia's devastated infrastructure. After erecting the primary bridging unit, they had spent the following day adding planking on either side of the bridge's single lane for pedestrian crosswalks.

Now they were back to finish off the job. Mansfield had come in his armoured vehicle, with a dozen engineer soldiers and more supplies in trucks behind him. They arrived to find a patrol of infantry soldiers from the Airborne's 2 Commando already waiting for them, wearing rueful expressions. The bridge had been completely stripped of everything that could possibly be pulled off. The frame and the main vehicle lane remained, but the nearly completed pedestrian crosswalks had vanished.

"It was like this when we got here," the Airborne sergeant reported. "They stripped it in the night."

The two Canadians stood there watching the locals file back and forth over the remaining centre lane of the bridge, apparently indifferent to the Canadian soldiers' presence.

Mansfield kicked the metal frame of the bridge with the toe of his combat boot. "Well, they aren't going to carry away this. I guess we'll have to leave it at that.

But the Canadians didn't leave it at that. They found other projects to work on in the area. One of the most important of those was working on schools. Education is the future, and one of the symptoms of the desperate state into which the local area had sunk was the fact that every single school in the area had been closed. Some had been heavily damaged in shootouts; all had been looted and stripped. After the bridge incident, Mansfield had thought he was prepared for anything, but even he was surprised to see the effort that had gone into stripping the local schools. Someone had gone so far as to rip the electrical wiring from the very walls. *It was probably old 1950s or 1960s era cabling,* he reflected. But still, it could be sold for a few pennies in the market places of Mogadishu. That was how desperate the locals were.

Determined to do what they could to break this cycle of poverty and desperation, the Canadians decided to open the schools in the Belet Huen area again. While Canadian headquarters concentrated upon canvassing the area for former schoolteachers willing to work for food, engineers concentrated on the practical job of making the school buildings usable. The leader for this task was Mansfield's second-in-command, an intelligent, energetic young officer, Captain Barbara Pierce.

The school building was no more than a wrecked shell. Pierce and her crew poked around it, scoping out the work. The half dozen Canadian engineers had arrived with a truckload of supplies and a section of Airborne soldiers with them for local security. They shouldered their weapons and seated themselves discreetly in the background. Pierce adjusted her sunglasses, squinting in the bright sun at the scene in front of her.

Several dozen Somali men, colourful clothes flapping on their emaciated frames, swarmed over the site. The agreement was that the locals would do the work. The Canadians were just there to provide the supplies and expertise.

"All right," Pierce said to her sergeant. "Have them get the stuff off the back of the truck. I'm going inside to check around."

Sergeant Ryall, Pierce's NCO in charge for this undertaking, nodded. "I'll get 'em to pile it up over there."

Soon the sergeant and his men had the Somalis streaming back and forth between the truck and the school building. Supplies began to pile up: sacks of cement, bricks, and — most precious of all in that arid and nearly treeless place — planks of lumber.

Pierce stood inside and looked over the rooms. It was a simple building. The roof was completely gone, but the building was divided into two large rooms that had likely been classrooms. The place had obviously been looted several times over, and lived in by squatters for a while. At the back was a smaller room, what must have been a washroom, now completely stripped of toilet, sink, and even pipes. Pierce walked over and peered more closely at this room. She could see marks on the wall where the pipes had been. *We can't replace the pipes,* she thought. *They'll have to use an outhouse out back. Just like an old one-room schoolhouse.*

When she emerged from the building, the Somali workers were well into the unloading job. They seemed in high spirits, shouting and laughing back and forth while they worked. Her men directed them with gestures and some basic words.

Pierce noticed some clan elders behind them, but not ones she recognized. Two older men stood there, with three young men behind them. The young men were impassive, stone-faced. But the two elders glared at the chaotic work scene with grim expressions. Pierce had seen that look before, and it didn't bode well at all.

It didn't matter whether it was building a bridge or repairing a school. As always in Somalia, the chief difficulty wasn't the engineering challenges. It was clan politics.

"What's up with them?" she asked Sergeant Ryall, gesturing over towards the new group.

"Don't know," Ryall replied. "They just showed up a moment ago. Haven't said anything, just stand there staring at us."

Pierce nodded across the yard to their translator, a local man hired by the Canadians, and waved him over. "Abdi! Come with me."

The gangly Somali, who had been translating one of the engineers' explanations of something to the workers, ran up and followed the Canadian captain over towards the newcomers.

"Abdi, do you know who they are?" Pierce asked.

"Oh yes, ma'am," the Somali said. "They are clan elders. They are leaders of the Hiwadle." The translator paused, then added. "I think they are not very happy."

Pierce sighed. "Why not, Abdi?"

"None of your men here are Hiwadle," the Somali said simply.

Pierce greeted the two elders and had Abdi explain what they were doing. The two elders looked the translator up and down silently for a moment before making any reply. Then one of them said a few words in the local dialect.

"They say this is not your school," Abdi translated.

"Of course it's not," Pierce said. "It's a Somali school. Tell them we are rebuilding the school for Somalis."

After this was translated the elder squinted at her, then asked another terse question.

"He asks, for which Somalis?"

Pierce looked directly at the elder. "The Somalis of Belet Huen. We want to rebuild all the schools here."

The elder gestured over at the workmen and said something else.

"He asks why we have none of his men here. These are all Heba Gebir. He wants to know where are the Hiwadle? Is this not for them, too?"

Both elders were now staring at her, distrust clear in their eyes.

"Of course it's for Hiwadle," Pierce snapped, growing

exasperated. Then she turned back to the translator and said, "Tell him, yes, it's for Hiwadle, too."

She glanced back at the three young men behind the elders while Abdi translated. They stood in a cluster, arms crossed over their chest, glaring at them. Pierce couldn't see any weapons, but they'd learned it was sometimes hard to tell.

Their security detail of Airborne troops had noticed the little discussion, too. The section commander came up beside Pierce, his rifle slung over his back, and nodded to the two elders. At that moment, a battered Somali pick-up truck came around the street corner and pulled up behind the three young men. Once again, they couldn't see any weapons on it, but Pierce didn't like the way things were developing. The pick-up had to be one of the "technicals," even if it was no longer obviously armed. Open carriage of weapons was now forbidden and the Airborne had confiscated many. But still, they all eyed the vehicle warily.

"Ask him if he objects to our being here," Pierce said to the translator. "Ask him if he doesn't want schools for their own children."

There was another exchange between their translator and the elder. Abdi seemed to be putting a fair amount of expressiveness into his side of the conversation, but the elder's responses were still terse.

"He says rebuilding schools is good, but wants to know why there are no Hiwadle."

"So where are his Hiwadle?" Pierce demanded. "Tell him

I am using the workers I was assigned. If he wants Hiwadle, ask him why he hasn't arranged it with our camp."

After another exchange in Somali, the translator said, "He says he will get workers from his clan. They come here."

Pierce turned to the Airborne section commander. "Can you raise zero?" she asked, using the radio call sign for base camp. "Ask them about the deal for the labourers, and tell them what's going on here."

The Airborne sergeant nodded and waved his radio operator over. Pierce turned back to the elders. "Tell him to bring his workers," she said.

After this was translated there was a nod from the elder and the technical roared off, gone, Pierce presumed, to pass on the message. The other workers, meanwhile, had finished unloading the truck and were now all squatting in front of the school, waiting for further instructions.

Pierce looked back at the two elders, who were still regarding them all impassively. The pick-up or technical or whatever it was had gone, so taking a deep breath she made a decision. "All right Abdi. Tell them I'm going to start work with the men I have now. If he arranges to get some Hiwadle workers here, they're more than welcome to join in when they get here, okay?"

"Yes, ma'am," the translator agreed. "I tell him."

To Pierce's relief, when given the news the elder simply pursed his lips thoughtfully and gave a taciturn nod. *It could be damn hard work helping these people,* Pierce thought.

* * *

During their time in Somalia, the men and women of the Canadian Airborne Battle Group rebuilt and reopened four schools in the Belet Huen area, another small part of the mission to not only bring stability to the area and ensure the distribution of humanitarian aid, but to jump start the process of rebuilding the nation itself. They also reconstituted a police force, something the area had been completely without before their arrival. The Canadian soldiers trained 185 new Somali policemen and, for as long as they were there, brought them along on their patrols with them. Clan fighting subsided, gun fights petered out, aid poured in, and life returned to the area.

Chapter 5
Somalia — Don't They Know This is a Hospital?

Another soldier who had been on one of the first Hercules transport aircraft into Belet Huen, not knowing what he was getting into, was Corporal Mario Charette. Charette was a young medic who had been attached to the Airborne for the mission in Somalia at the last moment. On New Year's Eve, 1992, rather than celebrating with his fiancé and friends as planned, he had found himself flying across Europe. From 30,000 feet he had seen the fireworks going off in Paris. His first destination in Africa had been Nairobi, Kenya, where the troops were put up at an impressive four-star hotel. *Not so bad*, Mario thought. But that last taste of luxury was just a one-night stopover. Next thing he knew, he was wedged into the cramped cargo bay of the Herc, sitting in an uncomfortable folding seat in between pallets of military gear. Airborne's 2 Commando had already arrived in Belet Huen and secured the immediate perimeter of the airfield, but there was still concern about the danger of incoming mortar rounds and rockets, or sporadic sniper fire. As a result, Hercules aircraft were making "hot landings," which meant no engine shut-down and no waiting around.

In the back of the aircraft it was hard to hear over the roar of the four turboprops, but everyone felt the massive jolt as they touched down on the dirt airstrip and the engines reversed thrust to bring them to a stop as quickly as possible. Suddenly, as the plane was still taxiing, the rear ramp yawned open. Immediately they were engulfed in thick, red dust. Visibility was near zero.

"Go! Go! Go!" the loadmaster yelled, barely audible over the roaring engines. "Offload! Offload!"

Mario grabbed what he could and frantically deplaned. He stumbled towards the open ramp with his pack and a duffle bag, and more kit being shoved into his arms as the soldiers offloaded the plane on the double. In a blur, kits and packs were passed from hand to hand and stacked at the side of the dirt runway, the plane's massive props still deafening and churning up thick dust that turned the whole world red. As Mario helped stack kit, he looked up to see the Hercules turning, the hydraulics pulling up the rear ramp while the aircraft was still moving. While he watched, the plane gained speed back down the runway and lifted off, heading back for another load.

Ears still ringing, Charette turned to get his first good look at his new surroundings. It was difficult for him to see through the swirling air, but as he moved along in the same direction as the rest of the soldiers, the village of Belet Huen came into view: mud huts, surrounded by livestock and small children; a few buildings lining the main road that crossed the village. To Mario it looked primitive, but not war-torn.

Where were the starving thousands that the mission was here to save?

* * *

Mario Charette hadn't expected to be deploying to the Horn of Africa, that January of 1993. He had just been assigned to the 2nd Field Ambulance, which was the Army's MASH-like field medical unit for the 2nd Brigade, located just north of Ottawa at Canadian Forces Base Petawawa. He had been thrilled with this assignment because he had grown up in nearby Gatineau. His sweetheart Genevieve still lived in the quiet little Quebec town, as did his family. A posting to Petawawa meant that he would be within driving distance of everyone he loved. At 26, Mario had spent four years training as a medic, and had just recently made corporal. Newly promoted and newly arrived in Petawawa, his ambition was to convince Genevieve to marry him, which he thought would make his life perfect.

That plan, however, would have to be delayed. Even though he had returned from the first Gulf war only 18 months earlier, just before the Christmas holidays he'd been ordered to join the Airborne for the deployment to Somalia. He didn't even have his parachute jump wings, but that didn't matter. The Canadian Forces were scrambling to deploy a unit to Somalia, and for this mission the Airborne would be deployed on the ground anyway. He was on his way to Africa.

Mario had spent his pre-embarkation leave wondering if the time was right to propose to Genevieve before he left. But she surprised him and beat him to the punch, asking him the question herself. Newly engaged, he found himself bidding an emotional farewell to his family and friends. But like the other soldiers deploying, he was excited. On television he had seen dramatic images of the trouble that Somalia was in, and he was eager to help.

After his arrival in Belet Huen, he quickly settled down to his routine as a medic. Belet Huen was not over-run with starving masses, like the most dramatic images they had seen on television, but it *was* destitute and suffering. There were no infrastructure or hygiene facilities. And medics were kept busy with local health hazards. Deadly snakes and insects joined the soldiers as they slept at night, and many of the peacekeepers were diagnosed with malaria, dengue fever, and dysentery during the course of their deployment.

The austere conditions, however, weren't the only danger the Canadians faced. Small-arms fire and mortar rounds plagued them night and day. When the locals ran out of shells, they pelted the soldiers with stones and rocks. Supplies disappeared on a regular basis because of theft by the local Somalis. The days were long. Soldiers worked from sun up to well beyond sun down — usually about 18 hours in total. But the mission was important to the Canadians. There were lives to be saved.

* * *

People who find themselves in horrific situations don't think about how their actions will be seen as heroic. For Mario this was certainly the case. When he found himself at the local hospital in Belet Huen on February 17, 1993, he never expected to end the day as a hero. He had merely decided to go along with the Canadian surgeons as a chance to improve his medical skills. He never anticipated having his life and the lives of an entire hospital full of people at stake. But Mario was about to save hundreds of lives.

On the day in question, Mario was asked to escort the Canadian surgical team to the makeshift hospital where the Canadian surgeon often accompanied the Somali doctors on their daily rounds. The hospital was in a run down old building with little medical equipment and less hygiene, but it was in a walled compound for its own security. A brick wall about nine feet tall, with shards of glass embedded in the top, served to dissuade anyone from climbing over the top. The only entrance into the compound was a metal gate, which the Somalis kept guarded and locked.

The Airborne medics often went with the Canadian doctors when they visited the local hospital. It was a chance to help out with the "hearts and minds" approach, and a chance for the medics to broaden their medical skills, too. Additionally, Mario would be responsible for making hourly radio checks back to base camp. The situation was still volatile enough that it was important to let others know where they were at all times.

The morning at the hospital passed routinely. Then, one of the nurses from the Red Cross invited Mario and his partner over for lunch at their location. After checking in with the Canadian surgeon, Mario offered to take them all in their jeep. Loaded down with the nurse and a few other civilian Red Cross workers, they made their way through town towards the Red Cross building.

But when they got to the small bridge in the centre of town the engineers had laid, they were stopped by Canadian troops. A riot had broken out on the other side of the bridge and shots had been fired. There was no way they'd be able to get through to the Red Cross location for lunch. They could go back to the hospital or back to the Canadian camp. Since they had left the surgeon at the hospital, they decided to return there.

When they pulled back into the hot dusty hospital compound, the Somalis slammed the gate shut behind them. Mario raised base camp on the radio to report their arrival and get an update on the overall situation.

The riot had spread. Just as he signed off, a crowd surged up to the hospital gate. And, more disturbingly, they noticed a few Somali men inside the compound carrying Kalishnikov assault rifles. That was highly unusual.

Slinging his own weapon over his shoulder, Charette approached the gunmen to find out what was going on. One of the ragged looking group of four youths informed him, in broken English, that they were there to protect the hospital.

"I see," Mario responded, eyeing them doubtfully. He heard the sounds of rioting outside the compound grow louder. So apparently, did the gunmen, who kept glancing nervously over towards the gate.

"Well," Mario went on, "this is a hospital, yes? You should put your weapons away."

The Somali shook his head vigorously, and there was a brief exchange amongst them in their own tongue.

"There are Canadian soldiers here," Mario said. "We will protect the hospital." He wasn't sure how much of this was getting though, so he thumped himself on the chest and gestured back towards the jeep. "Canadian soldiers," he repeated. Then he pointed to their weapons. "You put your weapons away. Hospital. No weapons."

The Somali who seemed to speak some English shook

his head again, and their tempers appeared to be rising. "No!" the Somali said. "No us. You!"

Suddenly, without warning, one of the Somalis leaped towards him, a machete raised to slash. Fortunately for Mario, the Somali who had spoken the broken English halted his attacker.

"Hey!" Mario yelled. "What are you doing? We're protecting your hospital!"

"We protect, too," the one Somali said. "Our hospital. No stop us."

Charette's eyes flicked over at the Somali with the machete. But they were no longer looking at him. They were now all looking over at the hospital gate, which they could hear the crowd pounding upon. It was rocking back and forth. Mario wondered how long it would last.

Things seemed to be spinning out of control. The Red Cross nurse appeared beside him, begging to be taken back to their station. "It's not safe here, its not safe here," she kept repeating. "I have to get back."

"We can't get back! We have to wait until the riot's over! Besides," Mario hollered, "there's no way I'm opening that gate!"

"Well, what are you going to do?!" she demanded.

Mario glanced over towards the Somali gunmen. They seemed to have forgotten him and had run over to the gate, which was shaking under the pounding. The shooting and yelling from the other side was growing louder and louder.

Mario did the only thing he could think of. He took the portable radio out of the back of the jeep. Yelling over the noise in the compound, he sent their base a situation report, hoping they would have some good news for him. The signal was weak and distorted and he could barely hear over the screaming and yelling. He moved over to a spot near the gate, where the reception seemed marginally better.

Suddenly, they all jumped as if slapped. A barrage of machine gun shots ripped out, deafening in the enclosure of the compound. One of the Somali gunmen had opened a small side door beside the gate and begun firing wildly into the crowd. He appeared to be trying to hit a member of a rival faction who was hiding in a small café on the other side of the street.

"What?!" Mario shouted, dropping the microphone.

"He's shooting!" the nurse yelled. "He's shooting!"

The crowd outside was thrown into complete hysterics. Charette later described them as "like a bee's nest stirred up with a stick." The rival faction began firing back. The gunman slammed the side door shut again.

Chaos was everywhere. Mario huddled the nurse close to him, shielding her with his own body. He fumbled with the microphone and tried to get through on the radio again.

Suddenly there was a deafening explosion and dirt and debris rained down around them. A grenade had gone off just on the other side of the wall. His mind racing, Mario put his arm around the nurse and tried to focus on the radio.

He kept repeating his call sign into the microphone but the coms were terrible. When he did manage to get through, he reported shooting and grenades at the hospital.

Still huddled over with his back to the courtyard, he felt a hand grasp his shoulder. He swung around to see another Canadian soldier.

Corporal Dwayne Atkinson, a mechanic from the maintenance platoon, had been working on the hospital's generator at the rear of the compound, originally oblivious to the chaos because of the noise of the generator. But when the grenade went off, that noise had penetrated. He had come running, finding Mario and the nurse kneeling close to the wall beside the gate. Mario was overcome with relief. Here was a fellow Canadian soldier. He wasn't alone.

"What happened, man?" Atkinson demanded.

"Grenade!" Mario yelled back. "And they're shooting too!"

"Look at that!" Atkinson pointed at the gate, still shaking from the enraged crowd on the other side.

"We've got to get her out of here!" Mario said, pointing at the nurse. "She's freaking right out!"

"Get her inside!" Atkinson yelled. "I'll watch the gate!"

Mario grabbed the nurse around the shoulders and ran for the hospital's door, bent over double. Panting, they burst through the door to find some of the Canadian medical staff inside, crouching down.

"What's going on out there?" they demanded.

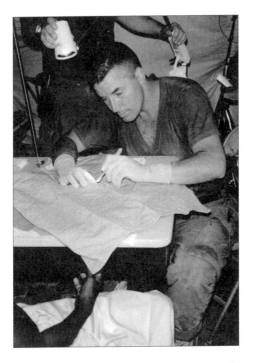

Cpl Mario Charette performing minor surgery on a Somalian.

"I've got to go back for Dwayne!" was all Mario could think to say. "I'll be right back!"

At the gate, the noise was still overwhelming. He decided to risk peeking through the side door, and he caught a glimpse of the chaos outside. People were screaming, running in circles, and yelling. Some lay in pools of blood. Some were wounded; others lay dead.

The crowd began to rush the small door, trampling over

the injured as they ran. The gunmen seemed to have disappeared, or at least, Mario had no idea where they were in the chaos. Injured people — people who needed immediate care — were everywhere.

"We've got to do something!" Mario yelled to Atkinson.

"What?" Atkinson yelled back.

"First aid! Let the wounded ones in!"

Atkinson planted himself at the door where he could control the flow of people surging in. But as quickly as it had begun, the fighting and rioting seemed over. Charette began to triage the wounded. But the area now overflowed with wounded. Soon the small compound was packed with bleeding Somalis and their friends and family.

The Canadians who had taken shelter inside the hospital building admitted the wounded for treatment. Mario rushed from casualty to casualty in the hot, dusty compound. The next several hours passed in a blur. He saw bodies stacked on stretchers, blood running away into thick dark pools from the ones who didn't make it. Many others he bandaged and helped save. The gunmen never did come back. To this day Charette has no idea what happened to them, or why they disappeared as quickly as they had appeared. In Somalia it was just like that.

Mario is modest in recounting the incident. He feels he was just in the wrong place … at the right time. Others saw it differently. With chaos exploding around him, he kept his cool, protected the hospital, and seized control of the situation to start aiding the injured, many of whose lives he saved. The Somali community was genuinely appreciative, too. The aid the Canadians provided to the many Somali injured that day was part of what established the good relations with the local clan leaders.

Corporal Mario Charette was presented the Medal of Bravery at Rideau Hall during the Governor General's awards ceremony on June 17, 1994, by the late Ramon John Hnatyshyn. Corporal Dwayne Atkinson received a Chief of the Defence Staff commendation.

* * *

The Canadian mission to Somalia has been widely misunderstood. It was never a peacekeeping mission. It was a difficult and dangerous peace enforcement mission, carried out under the most adverse of circumstances. Despite all of this, the Airborne Battle Group succeeded in stabilizing the area and bringing in aid to end the famine. More than that, they made real progress towards the long work of nation rebuilding.

The formal thanks to Canada from the Coalition commander stated:

One of the very striking successes was the Canadian Airborne Regiment's focus on civic action programs designed to improve conditions for the Somali communities within the Belet Huen sector. The Airborne Regiment took on the most ambitious program of any of the sectors with respect to the school reconstruction program.

But probably the best testament comes from the Somalis themselves. Abdi Osman Farah, a local official, wrote:

The people of the Hiran region did not know anything about Canada before your forces arrived in the city of Belet Huen and now all the children of the Hiran region are writing on the walls of the cities the name of Canada with charcoal. In addition, we have received countless appeals from the people of the region to ensure you stay in the region.

General Hubero, leader of the largest clan militia in the area, summed it up even more succinctly:

The Canadian Forces have done more for our region in five months than the previous two regimes in 30 years.

Chapter 6
Rwanda —
Screaming into
the Void

Silhouetted on the skyline, the Church of Sainte Famille rose on a gentle hill. In better times, the hymns of the faithful would have floated across a waking city. But on May 1, 1994, in the midst of the genocidal storm that had become Rwanda, only the sound of exploding mortars punctuated by the screams of the dying were heard over the radio net that General Dallaire, newly promoted to major general, was now monitoring.

It was early evening and the general was in his cramped office, working on stacks of paperwork when the radio call came in. A request for medical help was being relayed over the radio net. The church, which had become a refuge for thousands of desperate Rwandans, was now being shelled.

Grabbing his blue helmet and flak jacket, Dallaire ran down the hall, yelling for his driver. He needed to get there immediately.

It took over 30 minutes for General Dallaire to arrive at the church compound, and by the time he arrived, mercifully the shelling had stopped. But hundreds of panicked Rwandans were still trying to seek cover in the church, pushing against each other in a frenzied human mass. In the midst of the terrorized Rwandans, a handful of the general's blue bereted military observers were trying to calm the people down and assist the Red Cross workers with the injured and dying. It was a chaotic scene.

Quickly, Dallaire dismounted from his vehicle only to be swarmed by frantic families. Sobbing, they begged for his protection. Offering small words of comfort, Dallaire pushed his way through the screaming crowd and tried to assess the situation. In the middle of the courtyard, large craters had been created where the shells had hit. Scattered amongst them, people lay dying. It was a horrific scene, made worse by the smell. General Dallaire would later describe it as being the smell of burnt explosives mixed with burning blood and flesh. *Surely,* he briefly thought, *this is what hell must be like.*

The general pressed his way over to where some of the elders were trying to calm the people. He needed to console these people, yet what words of reassurance could he offer?

"Why weren't soldiers there to protect them?" they cried.

"Why did the world not care about their fate?" they wailed.

"Where was the UN?"

And for Dallaire, there was no answer he could give them.

* * *

The terrible genocide and civil war in Rwanda is difficult for most outsiders to fathom. Like many other places in the world, Rwanda is a mixture of different peoples. The two primary groups call themselves the Tutsi and the Hutu. Although there was little, if any, real difference between the two groups, they had increasingly come to see themselves as distinct. By the early 1960s, ethnic violence between Hutus and Tutsis had already become common, both in Rwanda and in the nation of Burundi, which lay just to the south of Rwanda. At that time, many ethnic Tutsis fled to neighbouring Uganda. In 1973, Juvénal Habyarimana, a Hutu, seized power in a coup. Hutus also seized power in Burundi. Habyarimana originally promised to end the ethnic strife, but the situation had polarized and most in either group distrusted the other.

Habyarimana made Rwanda an increasingly authoritarian, one-party state. The Tutsis who had fled to exile in Uganda formed a rebel faction that they christened the Rwandan Patriotic Front, or RPF. In 1990, open civil war broke out between Habyarimana's Hutu dominated regime

and the mainly Tutsi RPF. The forces of the Hutu-domi-
nated Habyarimana regime were known as the Rwandan
Government Forces or RGF.

On August 8, 1993, a peace agreement between the two
sides was finally reached, promising an integration of both
Hutus and Tutsis into one Rwanda. Known as the Arusha
Accords, after the Tanzanian city where it was signed, it was to
oversee this agreement that United Nations Assistance Mission
for Rwanda (UNAMIR) was established. The Arusha Accords
provided for a cease-fire and power-sharing arrangement
between the Hutu dominated RGF and the rebel Tutsi RPF.

* * *

But in the summer of 1993, then-Brigadier General Roméo
Dallaire had no idea what complex problems were wracking
the tiny land-locked African nation of Rwanda. As he has
freely admitted, he couldn't even have told you exactly where
Rwanda was. "Rwanda? That's in Africa isn't it?" were his
words when first offered the position of military commander
for the UNAMIR mission.

Seconded to the United Nations, this would be Dallaire's
first actual peacekeeping tour, although as commander
of the Quebec and Eastern Canada based 5th Canadian
Mechanized Brigade Group, he had overseen the preparation of numerous contingents for other peacekeeping missions. A dedicated officer who took the military ethos of the

profession of arms seriously, Dallaire felt this would be an interesting opportunity to add to his command experiences. What he didn't realize at the time was that the rest of his life would become deeply intertwined with the fate of the beautiful African country he would come to both love and hate.

UNAMIR was conceived as a classic peacekeeping operation. Active conflict had for the most part petered out, and with the signing of the Arusha Accords there was a peace deal in place to which both sides had agreed. In fact, the primary mission for UNAMIR was to simply observe the ceasefire and monitor the implementation of the accord. Many of UNAMIR's soldiers would not even be armed. It was the type of UN mission that Canadian peacekeepers had been excelling at for the past 40 years, and it was this type of mission that Dallaire and his small headquarters staff expected to be in charge of. General Dallaire would serve as the military force commander.

Problems for Dallaire and his staff began early. He had taken a reconnaissance trip to Rwanda in mid August 1993, so he could provide the United Nations with a technical report on the situation as the basis for drawing up the mission plan. One of the most serious issues was the fact that no world power was willing to come forward to lead the mission, except Belgium. As one of Rwanda's former colonial masters, this was not an acceptable solution for anyone. It seemed that the world wanted troops on the ground there, but no one wanted to supply them. With the crises in Yugoslavia and

Somalia flaring to their worst at that time, a small land-locked country that held no strategic value, like Rwanda, was not a priority for the UN's Directorate of Peacekeeping Operations. In an aside from a UN official, Dallaire was told to make the mission "small, cheap, short and sweet."

General Dallaire was forced to compromise. Instead of requesting resources for the mission, he was forced to plan the mission around the resources available. And not many resources were available. He was given half of the number of troops he calculated he would need, and very few supplies. He had requested 20 armoured personnel carriers but only eight were delivered, and only five of the eight actually ran. No mechanics were provided, no parts were issued, and the instruction manuals were written in Russian. Road vehicles came in without windshield wipers, and some were even missing seats. He requested ammunition, heavy weapons, and mortars, but all were denied.

The situation for the troops he did have was even worse. A miscellaneous collection of Bangladeshi, Ghanaian, and Tunisian soldiers were assigned to the mission, and these showed up on the ground with little more than their own personal kits. Mostly, they arrived with no vehicles, no communications, no logistics, and no support. Dallaire had no billets in which to house them and very little in the way of resources to supply them. UNAMIR did not even have field kitchens with which to feed them. But the worst was yet to come.

The United Nations Security Council officially approved

UNAMIR on October 5, 1993, and General Dallaire was anxious to get started. Within weeks, his small staff had settled in to the Amahoro sports stadium in the east end of Kigali. Amahoro meant "peace" in Kinyarwanda, Rwanda's local tongue, and the facility was a large complex consisting of a sports stadium, training facilities, and an athletes' hotel. It wasn't ideal but it would have to do.

Later in the month of October, Dallaire arrived in the country to assume formal command of the mission. As contingents of UN troops arrived, Dallaire was quickly caught up in a blur of meetings to attend, VIPS to greet, and a mission to get up and running. He would have to assess the country's humanitarian, political, and administrative needs, as well as the military ones, and report everything back to the United Nations headquarters in New York.

The misty mountains of the Rwandan countryside were lush and beautiful, but the country remained on the verge of civil war. Almost immediately after his arrival, General Dallaire began to face unexpected problems. In mid-November he caught the first hints of the trouble that was to come. Tension was building on Rwanda's southern border after a coup in neighbouring Burundi in which Tutsis had murdered the Hutu president. In response, Hutus began killing Tutsis. The vicious cycle of revenge and counter-revenge began spiraling out of control. Soon, streams of refugees were clogging the roads into Rwanda. The tiny UNAMIR mission was unequipped for literally hundreds of thousands of refugees, but soon even more worrisome developments came to light. News of isolated massacres of small numbers of civilians began to come in.

The massacre of the children in the Virunga mountains was but one of these reports. Massacred civilians are all too common in strife-torn refugee areas, but something about these reports wasn't right. The Tutsi RPF rebels were blaming the government RGF forces, and vice versa. But neither explanation seemed to fit the facts and Dallaire couldn't pin down the problem. It was almost as if a mysterious third force was moving about the country, killing innocent civilians at every turn. Dallaire and his soldiers were helpless in the wake of such atrocities — he simply did not have the manpower to cover the 10 provinces of Rwanda.

Worst of all was the message these murders were sending to the people of Rwanda. It was an immediate and deliberate challenge to the United Nations mandate. Yet General Dallaire could do nothing.

Neither was the peace process advancing well. No real progress was being made on power sharing between the Hutus and the Tutsis, and the sporadic killings continued. In early December, Dallaire received an unsigned letter warning that the peace process was about to be sabotaged. The anonymous letter claimed that people close to President Habyarimana were undermining the deal and planning to do something dramatic to overthrow the peace treaty. Tutsi lives would be at risk if this were to happen.

Then, Dallaire had a lucky breakthrough. An informant by the name of "Jean-Pierre" approached his staff and warned them of four weapons caches hidden around Kigali. The weapons were being smuggled into the city by the Interahamwe, the semi-official militia group run by Hutu extremists in the current government. Interahamwe was Kinyarwanda for "those who attack together," and hatred for their Tutsi neighbours was well entrenched in their radical doctrine.

But at first Brigadier General Dallaire was elated. In the form of Jean-Pierre, he thought he had finally found an answer to the mystery of the mysterious "third force" that was operating around the country. Jean-Pierre proved to be a highly reliable source. He had served as an officer in the Presidential Guard and now was the chief trainer of the Interahamwe. He told Dallaire not only of the weapons caches, but he also told of more sinister developments. Lists were being made around the country, lists of all Tutsis. These were being collected in every village and town, across the entire country. They were made in preparation for a great rounding up of all the Tutsis in the country at the right moment. They were death lists. Death squads were being formed and were training to carry out the killings. AK-47 assault rifles, ammunition, and grenades were being hidden in Kigali. Genocide was being deliberately, purposefully planned.

As part of the peace process, both sides had signed an agreement to keep Kigali a Weapons Secure Area. The weapons caches were a clear violation of the agreement. And the arming of the militia youth was an even more serious violation of the Arusha Accords themselves.

* * *

Grimly, Dallaire realized what had to be done. He and his staff resolved to act before the weapons could be used.

Dallaire and his military aide Major Brent Beardsley, another Canadian army officer, worked feverishly through the night. Dallaire was convinced that this was the chance to seize the initiative. It was January 10, 1994, and they had worked out a detailed plan for UNAMIR's troops to sweep in, collect the weapons, and disarm the militia. Now, convinced that the way ahead was clear, they were working on the final technicality. They drafted a fax, outlining their plan to UN headquarters in New York. Dallaire addressed it to the military advisor to the secretary-general and head of the military division of the Department of Peacekeeping Operations. By coincidence, this was a fellow Canadian army officer, Major-General Maurice Baril, an old colleague of Dallaire's, and an officer who would later rise to become the Canadian Chief of the Defence Staff.

Dallaire read the fax over one last time, and then impulsively added in his own hand at the bottom "*Peux ce que veux*" — a French expression meaning, more or less, "Where there's a will there's a way" — and signed with the salutation "*Allons-y*," which was the motto of his and Baril's old brigade

— "Let's Go." They fed the paper into the fax machine and, convinced that they had a sound plan and a clear way ahead, went to catch a little much needed sleep.

Dallaire could not have been more stunned by the response from New York. A cable arrived from Kofi Annan, the Under-Secretary General for Peacekeeping Operations (who would later become the Secretary-General of the United Nations), taking Dallaire to task for even thinking about touching the weapons cache. He was reminded of his restrictions as the mission's force commander. Not only that, but in order to avoid even the appearance of "spying" on one of the parties to the peace accords, New York ordered them to give all the information they had collected on the Interahamwe over to President Habyarimana and his staff.

It was a crushing blow. Wasn't New York able to grasp the seriousness of the situation? But Dallaire wasn't about to give up. He was convinced that he had a sound plan that could make a difference, and he and his staff kept up a barrage of reports and almost daily phone calls to New York. On January 21, he fired off a second fax, requesting permission to attempt a modified plan to seize the weapons. Always the answer was the same: No.

The situation in Rwanda, meanwhile, was going from bad to worse. Tension was everywhere and the national (Hutu controlled) radio station had begun broadcasting unremitting propaganda calling for Tutsi blood. Other things began to unravel, too. In anticipation of a worsening situation, Dallaire had requested supplies to prepare full defences for his forces, materials such as sandbags and reinforcements to build trenches and bunkers for his troops' positions. No defensive supplies arrived. His requests for additional troops were denied. No one was coming to augment his small contingent of third world soldiers and the troops he had now were already overstretched and beginning to burn out. Small-arms fire and grenade explosions were becoming commonplace around the city at night, and the murders continued. The new RPF liaison officer to the mission had almost been assassinated. UNAMIR was coming under direct attack and Dallaire knew he needed to do something to regain the advantage.

On the last day of January, Dallaire, now promoted to major general, decided to give it one last shot. He and Beardsley drafted yet another fax. This time, he included an extremely detailed assessment of the security implications of the situation. He explained in exacting detail how he would conduct the search and seizure of the weapons. He cited Arusha Article 54 — which gave him the necessary authority to conduct the operation. His plan was reasonable and carefully laid out. He knew that to allow those weapons to remain hidden in the militia's possession meant that innocent lives were at stake.

Dallaire later said that the answer he received from the UN three days later "whipped the ground out from under my feet." The response could not have been any blunter. "UNAMIR may provide advice and guidance for the planning of such operations, it cannot, REPEAT, cannot take an active role in their execution. UNAMIR's role should be limited to a monitoring function only." He had failed to convince the UN to act, and to this day this failure haunts him.

* * *

The mission, of course, continued, and Dallaire and Beardsley once again lost themselves in their work. Then, on April 6, 1994, the situation changed drastically and instantly. President Habyarimana's plane was shot down, killing him and all aboard. It is now clear that he was killed by Hutu extremists in his own government, probably because they feared he really was going to try and compromise with the Tutsis as the Arusha Accords required. Also, the extremists wanted to seize control of the government themselves and launch their genocide. Prime Minister Agathe Uwilingiyimana, a Hutu, was next in line to take power. But she was not an extremist, and the very next day she was killed along with her husband. Their children were saved by some of Dallaire's UN soldiers and safely evacuated.

Violence broke out everywhere all at once, exactly as the mysterious Jean-Pierre had warned. Interahamwe militia began rounding up their Tutsi neighbours. People were being killed everywhere. Ten peacekeepers from the Belgian contingent were caught by the militia and hacked to death. Women and children were killed, as militia members, often drunk, slashed them to death with machetes.

General Dallaire and the other UN soldiers found themselves personally swept into this chaos. The small peacekeeping contingent hunkered down in the sea of violence and did what they could, trying to escort threatened innocents to safer areas, guard key locations, or provide humanitarian assistance. But there was little they could do to deflect the course of events. It was a deliberate campaign of genocide, designed to "solve" the conflict once and for, by the simple expedient of killing all the Tutsis.

Much of this killing was especially sickening, even by the standards of ethnic cleansing, for most of the murders were committed by machete. Fields outside villages filled with the dismembered corpse of the local Tutsis. UN soldiers found churches and orphanages full of hacked bodies. Children, in particular, seemed to be deliberately targeted, as the Interahamwe tried to ensure no future generations of Tutsis would survive.

A few weeks later, on May 16, 1994, Dallaire was driving in his jeep, reflecting on everything that had happened since Rwanda's descent into the maelstrom of genocide. He felt the weight of the world on his shoulders that particular May day. The RPF wouldn't talk to him, and the Hutu government was accusing him of being pro-RPF. Just days earlier he had been warned by the Americans that an assassination was being planned against the "white man with the moustache." He now had two full-time bodyguards, sergeants from Ghana, along with a full section of soldiers as backup. But he was still the most vulnerable peacekeeper in the country. Threats against his life were even being broadcast across the national radio. As he drove past burnt huts with carrion birds overhead, he reflected on the irony of appearances. Even in May, with the rainy season over, everything was lush and verdant. The land looked like the Garden of Eden, but the blue-green beauty masked the true horror of the place.

He was on his way to the International Red Cross Hospital in Kigali. The Red Cross hospital was one of the only two hospitals in the area, and its services were desperately needed. But he had received word that Interahamwe militiamen were barring access. Driving up the steep hill to the hospital, his diesel engine announcing his arrival, the general was mad. Following behind him in their own jeep were his two Ghanaian sergeants, men so big and ugly that Dallaire's staff had affectionately nicknamed them the "motorcycle goons." They were shirtless but wore flak jackets over their dark, muscled torsos. A truck with the section of Ghanaian soldiers pulled up behind them.

For General Dallaire, Interahamwe's attempt to deny access to the hospital might have been the final straw. What right did these thugs have to deny women and children access to medical care? The Red Cross had always gone to great lengths to remain neutral, often to the consternation of others. These people were dirty, tired, and bleeding from the brutal gashes only a machete could make. They were scared and they needed help.

Dallaire leapt from his vehicle and stalked up to the leader of the ragged looking militia who were lounging and laughing around the hospital entrance, amusing themselves by terrorizing the people. The Ghanaian sergeants piled out behind the man they admired and respected so much that they called him "Father." They took up station on either side of the general, crossed brawny arms over their chests, and glared through their "trademark" mirrored sunglasses at the cocky leader of the Interahamwe militia. Even with the section of armed soldiers back at the vehicles behind them, they were still outnumbered and face-to-face with a group of thuggish, quite possibly drunken, murderous militiamen.

"What are you doing here?" Dallaire demanded.

"We are on security detail," the cocky leader of the militia soldiers responded. Behind him some of the other Interahamwe snickered and laughed amongst themselves.

"What concern is it of yours?" the militiaman demanded haughtily. "Go back to your UN place and leave us to take care of our business here." Behind him, Dallaire could hear some of the others take up their chant "Hutu Power! Hutu Power!"

Months of disheartenment and helplessness came bubbling to the surface. Dallaire had just seen too much; something in him snapped. His warnings and professional advice had been ignored. The genocide he had foreseen and warned of had swirled over the whole country, consuming literally hundreds of thousands of innocents. Everywhere he turned, he had been forced to accept that there was nothing he could do. But here, at this hospital, at this time, he could make a difference. Today he was not going to just be a witness to more atrocities.

Powerful with fury, he thundered, "Not here! Not now! Now pack up this riff-raff or I'll pack you off to Hell!"

In an instant, the militia's joking demeanour disappeared. Here was the general in person, the white man with the moustache, the officer the radio was inciting them to kill. The brash Interahamwe leader flicked his eyes from the inscrutable expressions of the sunglass wearing Ghanaian sergeants and then farther back to the five Ghanaian soldiers at the trucks. The blue berets were both out numbered and out gunned. But Dallaire's tired, red-rimmed eyes bore into them. He wasn't bluffing. The arrogant look of the young Interahamwe evaporated.

"*Oui. Oui, mon general ...*" the leader muttered. He gestured to the other men and sheepishly they disappeared into the crowd.

Relief crossed the dark faces of the Ghanaian sergeants. Satisfaction came over Dallaire's. It wasn't much. But it was *something.*

Chapter 7
Rwanda — The Most Vulnerable

Major Brent Beardsley lay alone, close to death. Pain and delirium were his only companions in the Nairobi hotel room as he drifted ever closer to the end, barely able to move. But when the phone rang he managed to drag himself out of bed to answer. It was his wife, Marge, calling from Canada. Hoarsely, Brent told her he was dying. Horrified, Marge made him promise to get to a hospital and then called the Canadian Forces Operations Centre at National Defence Headquarters in Ottawa. Frantically, she told them her husband was very ill and needed help. The duty officer contacted the Canadian air force detachment in Nairobi and Major Chuck Oliver rushed out to Brent's aid. After he recovered, Brent credited Major Oliver with saving his life. But how had

Brent had gotten so sick in the first place? And why was he all alone?

Just three days earlier, back at his post in Rwanda, Brent had begun to feel ill. He went to lie down during the day and had been found by Major General Dallaire. Dallaire was worried. Brent was always energetic — he never rested during the day. Something must definitely be wrong for him to take a rest, even for a moment. Brent told Dallaire he had a headache. By supper time, however, Brent was racked with pain and unable to move his fingers, consumed with fever. One of the UNAMIR staff, Captain Babacar Faye Ndiaye, recognized the illness as malaria and Dallaire immediately ordered Brent over to see the Ghanaian battalion's doctor, who had set up a treatment centre at the Kigali airport. Brent was diagnosed with malaria and administered a large quantity of medication. The doctor told him to go back to the headquarters and rest; he would feel better in a few days.

But instead of getting better, that night he grew much sicker. He was being given the malaria drugs every few hours throughout the night, but by morning he was so gravely ill that Dallaire ordered him to Nairobi for more thorough medical attention.

Doctors in Nairobi examined him and then placed him in a nearby hotel. Incredibly, he seems to have been overlooked or forgotten; two days later he was still alone there, literally dying. The fortunate fact that his wife called from Canada is the only reason he is alive today.

Major Oliver immediately had Brent evacuated back to Canada, where it was discovered that he was extremely allergic to the anti-malaria drugs he was being given. Brent's near-fatal reaction to them would take nearly a year of recovery back in Canada.

* * *

Losing Brent, Dallaire said later, was a crushing blow. They hadn't even had a chance to say a proper goodbye. Major Brent Beardsley, a calm and capable officer from the Royal Canadian Regiment, had been assigned with General Dallaire from the very beginning of the mission, as the general's military assistant. He would become his right hand man in all things Rwandan. For many hundreds of Rwandans, Brent would become their personal salvation.

While still setting up for the mission in Canada, Dallaire had been given a list of 10 officers from which to choose an assistant. Brent had come highly recommended, and that recommendation soon proved its worth. From the very start, he immersed himself heart and soul in the Rwanda mission. He believed just as passionately as Dallaire that UNAMIR must succeed — that the country could be saved. When it wasn't, he was just as devastated.

Brent grew up in Ottawa and Montreal, and then joined the Canadian Forces for the usual reasons — a challenge, travel, and a chance to serve for something he believed in.

One dramatic example of the sort of thing he was involved with in Rwanda came early in the mission, before the assassination of President Habyarimana and the genocide.

In January 1994, Brent was working late in the makeshift offices of UNAMIR's headquarters when a radio call came in. A mob was building outside the Rwandan National Assembly, known as the Conceil National Pour le Development or CND. It wasn't unusual for crowds to gather outside the CND, as it was the Rwandan equivalent of the parliament buildings. But this mob was different. It was armed. And the mood was growing ugly.

In response, Brent rushed out to his jeep with his Belgian driver, Master Corporal Troute. By the time they pulled up in front of the CND buildings, it was almost dark. They found a surreal scene: a seething crowd, chanting and surging back and forth, half seen in the dim light. Some of the people seemed to be injured. He and his driver pushed their way through to the official compound. There, guards told him the crowd had just killed a man. Brent told the guards to stay where they were; he would see what could be done. Turning back to the crowd, he and his driver began pushing their way through to see what was causing all the excitement. At the centre of the melée, they came upon a bleeding, heavily pregnant woman. The motionless figure of a man lay beside her, covered in blood. Brent could see wounds on his face and head that went to the bone. Machete wounds. That must have been the man who had been killed. After a cursory glance at the figure of the man, Brent turned to see what he might be able to do for the woman. She was terrified. Suddenly, the man at her side moved a little and groaned. He wasn't dead after all!

Almost without thinking, Brent picked up the blood-covered man and threw him over his shoulder. Behind him, his driver helped the woman up. But the next moment a man stepped forward from the swirling crowd to challenge Brent. In the dark, the Canadian officer couldn't see what he had in his hand, but he thought it must be a machete.

Deftly, Brent shifted the weight of the man slightly and leaned over to slug the troublemaker square on the jaw. Troute raised his rifle and the crowd moved back. Together, they hurried back to their jeep as fast as they could with the wounded couple, Troute continuing to wave his weapon at the crowd. They packed the two into the back of the jeep as quickly as they could and peeled off into the night.

At the King Faisal Hospital, a medical facility that had been donated by the Saudi Arabian government in more peaceful times, Brent and Troute handed over their patients to the staff. The woman had been inconsolable, nearly hysterical in the vehicle, but neither Brent nor Troute could understand her. Now, she was virtually screeching in Kinyarwanda. One of the hospital staff told them what she was saying. A child had been with the couple and had been torn from her arms. The crowd had the baby.

Standing in the hospital foyer, his front stained with

fresh blood, Brent was horrified. No wonder the woman was out of her mind with grief. She cared little for her own injuries. She just wanted her child. A father himself, Brent grabbed Troute and they raced back through the night to the CND. What were the chances after all this time of finding the baby alive, or even dead?

Brent's heart stopped when they arrived back at the scene. Almost worse than the swirling madness that had been there when they left, the courtyard was now empty. The silence and emptiness after the previous chaos was almost eerie. Where had such a crowd gone in such a comparatively short time? More to the point, where might a baby have gone? With a sinking heart, Brent and Troute looked at each other and the now empty scene. The two men stepped out of their vehicle and looked around in the dim light. Then, the peace-keepers noticed a figure in the shadows, against the wall. Approaching, the figure revealed itself as a woman. She was cradling a baby. Brent's heart leapt.

"Is this your baby?" he asked in his laboured French.

"*Non*," she replied, shaking her head. Their hopes soared.

"Is this the child of the woman who was injured?"

"*Oui*," she nodded.

Feeling almost supernatural relief, they brought her and the baby to the hospital. A week later, Brent checked back on the little family. He was heartened to see all three doing well. It was a small victory, but a victory nonetheless.

It wasn't to be Major Beardsley's only victory. A Protestant, his exploits in Rwanda saving the members of Catholic missions would earn him the tongue-in-cheek moniker of "military adviser to the Catholic church." Rwanda had no less than 15 religious orders with various missions working around the country in 1994. Canada's own Soeur de Bonne Pasteure had been ministering to both the Hutus and Tutsis since 1968. After the colonial period and the exodus of the Belgians, religious brothers and sisters had moved in to fill the humanitarian gaps. Brent would do to everything in his power to protect the men and women in these ministering groups.

* * *

Late evenings were busy for Brent. The time change between Rwanda and the rest of the world meant that when relatives and friends called to beg someone to check on or help their loved ones in Rwanda, the calls would come during the after-hours. It was not uncommon for Brent to spend hours scribbling notes on tiny pieces of paper, the name of this expat, the location of that stranded nun. Every evening the list would grow longer and longer and Brent often found himself planning more and more complicated rescue operations as the intensity of the genocide and civil war increased. He settled into a gruelling routine, taking phone calls by evening, and then travelling through contested battle lines and past blood crazed militiamen manning checkpoints by day. Danger was literally around each turn, and Brent knew that his blue beret provided little protection or, in many cases, even respect.

Like Dallaire, Brent had come to think of Rwanda as a land of dichotomies. The beauty of the countryside belied the nature of events there. The morning of April 16, 1994, a few weeks into the genocide, he found himself musing over these thoughts as he embarked on yet another rescue mission. Neat little terracotta huts blurred past him as he rode in a jeep with the Polish Captain Stefan Stec driving; a truck followed behind them with two more UN peacekeepers in the cab. Their little convoy was on its way to locate some stranded Canadian nuns.

The smell of burning wood was heavy in the air, but it could not conceal the smell of rotting human flesh. Earlier that week, Brent had ordered the killing of a dog that was pestering their compound. Much to everyone's horror, the soldier that had been tasked with the job returned to tell them the "dog" was actually a rat. His size and aggressiveness were the result of feeding on the abundance of human flesh that lay about everywhere.

For Brent, the smells of Rwanda would be one of the strongest memories he would take back to Canada. Even today, he cannot bear the smell of wood smoke. Fires were used to burn the bodies. As a result, smoke was ever-present in the air. "The smell of death was always there, always thick.

It gets inside your skin. You can taste it in your coffee," Brent would say years later.

But that morning he had more serious issues on his mind than the unavoidable stink. The prior evening he had received information that several Canadian nuns were stranded in their convent on the outskirts of town, which was behind several militia checkpoints. The mother superior was adamant that Major Beardsley get the nuns to the Kigali airport so they could be moved to safety.

Their rescue plan was straightforward enough. Travel to the convent and then bring the nuns back to the Kigali airport. It was only a week and a half since the mass killings had started, and movement around the capital was not yet as dangerous as it would later become.

As they travelled along the road to the convent, the trio saw that a militia roadblock had been set up at the intersection where they needed to turn into the convent. The Polish officer who was driving seemed to freeze. Instead of turning left into the convent he went rigid, gripping the wheel so hard his knuckles turned white at the wheel; he hit the gas and drove straight through the roadblock. Their truck following behind stopped before the intersection, waiting for them.

Brent realized what had happened. The day before Captain Stec had stopped at a roadblock and the Interahamwe had tried to drag a girl out of his vehicle. Gendarmes had stopped them, but Stec had vowed that he would never stop at a roadblock again. Unfortunately, the road behind the intersection they had raced through was a dead-end. They were now trapped behind the very checkpoint they had just raced through. Brent reassured the distraught Polish officer and calmly instructed him to reverse and head back. Tension rising, they executed a three point turn and headed back towards the checkpoint. With a gush of relief, they were waved through without comment; one could never tell what the militiamen were thinking.

Two minutes later, with heart rates just returning to normal, they arrived at the Convent of the Soeur de Pasteur. As their little convoy pulled up before the building, they were greeted by a bevy of nervous and excited nuns around the main door. Brent quickly informed the bewildered nuns that he was there to take them to safety. But after such a nerve wracking journey Brent was unprepared for their answer.

One of the nuns stepped forward and demanded, "Did the mother superior order us out or ask us to leave?"

Stalling for time, Brent asked her name.

"Sister Monique," she replied. "Do we have the choice to leave or not?" she persisted.

Brent realized he was faced with a moral dilemma that he'd been hoping to avoid. He was here to evacuate the Canadian nuns, but how could he do that and leave behind their Rwandan sisters, some of whom were bound to be Tutsi? On the other hand, what good would it do to leave the Canadian nuns there, too? They would scarcely be able to stop any militia that might show up to search the place, and if they protested or even just witnessed events, they might be attacked. Worse, he was still nervous about the checkpoint just down the road. If he tried to take the Rwandan sisters with him and the militia searched their truck and found the Rwandan women, who knew what they would do? Attack them all? Certainly they were likely to drag off any nuns they suspected of being Tutsi, whether they actually were or not. And the Rwandan nuns didn't even have passports, so what would they do with them, even if they got them out of the convent and to the airport? Without passports there was nowhere they could take them out of the country. Maybe the safest thing for them would be to stay in the convent. The genocidal rampage was only in its second week at this point, and they were still hoping that the situation could be stabilized. And so far, at least, the militia hadn't been attacking international institutions such as church compounds. All of this flashed through Brent's mind as the nun stared at him. And finally, he knew that if he hesitated too much, they wouldn't believe his answer.

Brent licked his lips and said, as firmly as he could, "Yes, of course. The mother superior orders all the Canadian nuns out. She is most concerned for all of your safety."

This provoked a flurry of reaction amongst the women, culminating in another demand from Sister Monique. "And what of our non-Canadian sisters? What of them?"

Brent glanced over the group. Fearful wide eyes in Rwandan faces stared back at him. His stomach churning,

Brent gritted his teeth and said, "My ladies, I'm afraid there is a checkpoint just a moment down the road. The safest thing for them would be to stay here, inside the convent."

Grudgingly, the Canadian nuns agreed to be transported away from their convent and on to the airport for evacuation. The decision made, a flurry of activity broke out around the vehicles as belongings were quickly grabbed, sobbing good-byes were said, and the Canadian nuns climbed into the back of their truck while the soldiers watched nervously over their shoulders towards the roadblock.

A short time later, their little convoy pulled out and headed back the way they had come, towards the checkpoint. Palms sweating, they slowed as they approached, but once again were waved through without incident. With relief they reached the airport and dropped the nuns off for a flight out of Rwanda. The airport was packed with Westerners scrambling to get out.

Later that day, Brent got a phone call from Nairobi. It was Sister Monique, now safely out with the rest of the Canadian nuns. But they hadn't called to thank him. In fact, Brent hadn't realized that women of God could get so angry and use such language. They had just found out that their mother superior *hadn't* actually "ordered" them out. After taking an ear-full, a chastened Brent agreed to look out for the convent and the remaining nuns, and provide them food and water. Feeling responsible, he took it on as his personal mission for the rest of his tour.

Major Beardsley and his team would try several times to move the Rwandan sisters, but to no avail. On April 29, on another trip back to the convent to drop off food and water, he found the place in an uproar. The nuns gathered around him, terrified. Interahamwe militia had come that very morning and hauled all the sisters into the courtyard, separating the Hutus from the Tutsis. Forcing them to the knees, the men from the militia began to taunt them that they were going to be killed. The sisters were scared, but put their trust in God. They began to pray together in the courtyard. Then suddenly, just at the moment they thought must be the end, the militiamen simply stopped and left without a word. The nuns believed it must have been a miracle.

Maybe it was a miracle. Maybe the sound of their prayers had unnerved the would-be murderers. Another possible explanation came in the arrival of a young Rwandan officer an hour or so later. He was from the regular army, not the Interahamwe, and he apologized for the behaviour of the militiamen. "I'm a good Catholic," he told the sisters. He pledged to look out for them.

A couple of weeks later, when the situation had deteriorated even further, that same young Rwandan army officer tried to take the nuns out himself. He placed them on a government truck and sent them on their way. However, by this point the Interahamwe militia were rampaging, and despite the fact that it was a Rwandan army truck, stopped them, separated the Tutsis from the Hutus and proceeded to massacre the Tutsi nuns. No one was able to save them this time, not even an officer of the Rwandan government's own army.

This story illustrates the sort of personal moral dilemmas that afflicted all of the UN peacekeepers in Rwanda, and torments many of them still. The best thing they could do, Major Brent Beardsley believed, was to remind themselves about whatever good they had managed to achieve in the midst of such horror.

Chapter 8
Rwanda —
This Must be Hell

The guard ordered brusquely, "You wait here." The guard eyed him suspiciously, and turned to call to someone. Captain Yves St-Denis shifted uneasily in the jeep's seat. He was one of the handful of Canadian officers who had recently arrived in Rwanda in response to General Dallaire's pleas for reinforcement. Out in the countryside for his first UNAMIR mission, the mood at the government checkpoint where they sat was growing hostile.

Captain Yves St-Denis, a logistics officer, had been working in the personnel field at National Defence Headquarters in Ottawa when his office received the request from Major General Dallaire. The Rwanda mission needed a logistics officer for a one-year tour. When St-Denis had difficulty finding someone willing to go to Africa for a whole year, he decided to submit his own name for the job. His family life was well settled and he wanted to get some UN experience. He felt the UN mission for Rwanda would give him that. And as a Francophone military officer in Rwanda (a nation that had been colonized by Belgium and thus spoke French), language would not be a hindrance. With great anticipation, he looked forward to his departure date, which was scheduled for early April.

Early April, of course, was exactly the time when the extremists murdered President Habyarimana and the genocide began. In the chaos, St-Denis's mission was put on hold for several weeks. Finally, in late April, he was given the go ahead and with a tearful goodbye, he began his long trek to the African country he knew very little about.

By the time he landed in Kigali on May 8, the situation had deteriorated to the point that civilian flights into the airport had almost ceased. He came on a Canadian CC-130 Hercules military transport aircraft and he, too, experienced the dubious pleasure of a "hot landing." He jokes that his luggage was literally thrown off the back of the Herc like supplies being para-dropped. That sense of urgency set the tone for his entire tour. On his way from the airport to mission headquarters at the Amahoro Stadium, St-Denis saw his first dead body. It was a shock, and at that moment he identified the smell hanging in the air.

On May 12, 1994, St-Denis and fellow Canadian new

arrival Captain Luc Racine were given their first assignment. They were to do a reconnaissance to the southern city of Butare, close to the Congo border. There was an airport there that could be used to move in desperately need supplies and reinforcements. Since the crisis had begun, no UN personnel had been able to get through to that particular area of the country, and General Dallaire wanted a report on the utility of the airport. The reconnaissance, or "recce" (pronounced "wrecky," and rhyming with Becky), as the military calls them, was to be straightforward. Essentially, they were to check on the airport and collect information on its usability and the route down. St-Denis was being sent for the job because these were primarily questions that a logistics officer could answer. St-Denis and Racine estimated that they could reach the border by nightfall, collect their information, and then promptly return.

Anxious to do well on their first operational mission, they set off early in the morning with a jeep. Right away, they realized it was not going to be a simple as they had thought. On the outskirts of Kigali they encountered some weapons fire, but passed it by. Every 10 kilometres or so they came across roadblocks, many with large numbers of Interahamwe militiamen hanging around them. Time and again they had to show their identification and explain the reason for their trip, while rough looking militiamen peered in their vehicle's windows. More often than not, the process was done at gun-point with hostile, angry youth on the other end.

The trip was an incredible revelation for the two newly arrived Canadians. Although surrounded by the lush green hills of the Rwandan countryside, the frequent roadblocks manned by hostile armed men gave a palpable sense of uncertainty to their trip. It took them all day to arrive at the first location — the small town of Butare.

St-Denis and Racine decided they would have to stop there for the night, so they found a local hostel and got themselves a room. As had been the case most of the way from Kigali, Butare seemed on edge. Why were people so scared?

Hoping to get some important information to take back with them, the two captains decided to visit the local police commander and then talk to the mayor. The mayor assured them that the massacres had not reached Butare and that the location was an oasis of calm amidst the storm. Uncertain, Racine and St-Denis decided to take a look around the town. As they travelled back towards the hostel, they managed to get stuck behind a dump truck.

Again, the pervasive, rotten smell struck St-Denis. They drove by people dressed in pink, who waved at them frantically. Later, St-Denis learned that they were prisoners who had spent the day being forced to clean up the dead bodies of the massacre. The mayor had lied to them. In fact, the mayor had been one of the main instigators of the Butare massacre and had played a leading role in the local genocide.

That evening back in their hostel, as the two officers tried to relax a bit in their spartan little room and take stock of what they had seen that day, they heard shouting coming from the lobby entrance. Someone was yelling that he wanted to see the Canadians in the hostel. Racine and St-Denis glanced apprehensively at each other, then took a deep breath and decided to go and see what the problem was.

Once downstairs, they found themselves confronted by an angry full-colonel from the Rwandan Government Forces, with a few of his bodyguards. Cautiously, Racine introduced himself to the irate colonel, and St-Denis attempted to make small chat with the bodyguards, but they were not willing to be won over by the French-Canadian's charm. They began to berate St-Denis about the war and to blame General Dallaire for the crisis.

Their logic was that since Dallaire had allowed the RPF representatives into Kigali, even though that was part of the power sharing deal in the Arusha peace accords, it amounted to the militia's bid for power. One of the bodyguards began to brag that he wished that he could get what he called a "crack" at Dallaire.

St-Denis tactfully tried to move the conversation away from Dallaire, but the bodyguard refused to change the subject. Belligerently, he began to quiz St-Denis about his own relationship with Dallaire. Fearing for his safety, St-Denis told the bodyguard that he knew little about Dallaire; at that time, this was true. But as both a UN and a Canadian officer, St-Denis felt that he should defend the general's honour, although the atmosphere was growing tense and menacing.

Under the circumstances, he felt it wise to try and remain nonchalant and neutral.

Eventually, the colonel and his bodyguards departed, but the incident had only served to underscore the tension of the situation they were now in. Before retiring for the night, St-Denis loaded his pistol and kept it close to the bed. A restless night followed.

The next morning, a pleading hostel manager approached the two Canadians. She was hiding a Tutsi family in her home but could no longer protect them. Could the Canadian UN officers do something with them? Take them away to safety? Protect them?

Both Racine and St-Denis were distraught. There was no conceivable way they could take the family on to the border. At the first checkpoint they would be found and pulled from the jeep. They were probably safer where they were. But that wasn't very safe, and it put the hostel manager and her family at risk if they were caught hiding them. What should they do? What could they do?

Feeling sick to their stomachs, the two Canadians apologized, promised to report what they could, paid their bill, and left. The plight of this family still weighs heavily on St-Denis's mind. But he saw nothing they could do to help. Later that day, they were to see more of just how true that perception was.

They reached their objective that afternoon, and after quickly making their survey they set off for the next airport they were to check out, which was in nearby Cyangugu. Government forces there were equally hostile and unco- operative. But the worst incident of their trip came on the return to Kigali. For some reason, a rumour began to circu- late amongst the Rwandans that General Dallaire himself was travelling with them. The Canadians were stopped at a checkpoint as the guards searched for the general. Unfortunately for St-Denis, he bears a certain resemblance to General Dallaire, including his mustache and French- Canadian accent. While they were sitting in their jeep at the checkpoint, St-Denis noticed one of the militia guards star- ing at him — closer and closer.

The guard demanded his papers, but even the three pieces of identification St-Denis produced did not seem to convince him. Leaving St-Denis squirming uncomfortably in his jeep, the guards called over their superior. The guard accused St-Denis of being the "white general with the mustache."

Again St-Denis produced his papers, but now the super- visor, too, was convinced that he had the UN commander at his checkpoint. St-Denis could feel panic rising in his chest. Fearing for his and Racine's safety, he put the jeep into gear and raised his weapon. Were the militiamen going to press the point in light of a loaded rifle? Would their first recce be their last?

Luckily, the raised weapon caused the supervisor to hesitate. St-Denis didn't waste a moment in seizing the opportunity. Placing his foot on the gas, he sped on past the checkpoint. With their hearts pounding in their throats, both Racine and St-Denis pledged that they were not going to stop for anyone until they reached the safety of the UN headquarters back in Kigali. The atmosphere in the country had become positively thick with menace.

* * *

It had become painfully clear what was happening in Rwanda. Now that the assassinated President Habyarimana and the moderate prime minister no longer stood in their way, the extremists had launched a terrible genocide. They had decided that they would simply kill every Tutsi in the country — as well as any Hutu moderates or anyone else who didn't agree with them or might stand in the way of their seizing power.

The primary instrument for this killing rampage was the Interahamwe militia, who had been set up in a vast network across the entire country. Now they roamed from house to house, village to village, rounding up those who were known to be Tutsi, or suspected of being Tutsi, or of sheltering Tutsis, or even of being moderate. When they realized what was happening, the rebel RPF army burst through their side of the cease-fire line, trying to capture the tiny nation and throw the extremists who had seized the government out of the country. Civil war had come back to Rwanda.

But most of the killing did not happen along the front

line, as deaths usually do when armies clash. The real genocide occurred in the rear areas of the country, perpetrated
mainly by the militia. Most victims were killed by machete, an
especially brutal method of slaughter. People from both ethnic groups were terrified. Many ran for their lives. Rampaging
and often drunken militiamen killed many, just because they
had their life savings with them, even if they were Hutu.
Rwanda had descended into a macabre hell.

* * *

The stench in the church was becoming overpowering.
Packed with refugees literally jammed on top of each other,
without adequate toilet facilities, let alone adequate wash-
ing facilities, hygiene had fallen by the wayside. But it was
more than just the sweaty smell of unwashed people, Captain
Andre Demers thought, as he surveyed the scene. Fear and
terror have their own rank smell, and it was thick on the hot
summer air.

Demers, a young infantry officer from the Van Doos, was
another of the small number of Canadians sent to Rwanda as
reinforcements to the UNAMIR mission, at the same time
as St-Denis and Racine. Since arriving in the country he had
been assigned to the humanitarian cell. Today he was visiting
the Ste-Famille church in the centre of Kigali. It had become,
like so many religious sites in Rwanda, a place of refuge, and
now it was packed with terrorized people. The church was so

full that the people could barely all sit down to eat, let alone sleep. The priest in charge had to tread a fine line between upholding his religious duties to his flock and avoiding an open breach with the Hutu extremist authorities. The nuns, undistracted by such concerns, were doing everything they could for the writhing pile of humanity in their care.

So far, at least, the militias roaming the streets of the city in ever-greater recklessness and blood lust hadn't dragged anyone off from the church, but the sounds of shooting and yelling coming from outside the church's walls were so terrifying that people huddled together in fear.

Demers had been put in charge of the small UN team that, along with UNICEF, brought in what food supplies they could manage to the group, a few times coming under sporadic weapons fire as the situation in the city deteriorated. Today however, despite the occasional shots they could hear in the distance, they arrived without incident. The Sister of Charity thanked them with heartfelt emotion when they arrived to unload a truck filled with high-energy biscuits for the children.

"More come every day," the nun said. "We have almost nothing here now. The Interahamwe are terrible." The nun's eyes flashed towards the sounds coming from outside the compound, then she looked back and smiled. "But God will protect us."

After that, they began organizing refugee convoys from the church. From various such safe havens that had spontaneously developed as refugee points — mostly churches or other religious sites, but also the now famous Hotel Milles Collines — UNAMIR began to arrange truck convoys to move the terrified people to refugee camps behind the front lines. By mid June, Demers had successfully made several convoy trips from the Ste-Famille church. Now, on June 13, he was back to make the next refugee convoy.

He pulled up to the large open area in front of the church in his white UN jeep, four large trucks with canvas-covered backs in convoy behind him. It was a fair-sized brick church, with a small courtyard out back. Before the genocide, Demers reflected, it must have been quite a lovely little green patch. Now it was trampled and packed with people. Dozens of faces, wide eyes in each, turned to regard him as he came to a stop. Coming down the steps of the adjacent rectory, Father Wenceslas, dressed incongruously in a military bulletproof vest with a pistol stuck in his waistband, greeted Demers. The good Father had been somewhat upset that people would want to leave his protection for the other side of the lines, but he had always accepted the UN's role in the transfers.

"Are they ready?" Demers asked, pulling out his sheaf of paper. The Rwandan authorities insisted they document everyone they moved as being under UN care. There was little guarantee the men on the roadblocks would respect the safety of their charges, but it was all they had to offer.

"They are ready," the priest said in his deep resonant

voice. It could be difficult for him preparing for these trips. Some people were too terrified to leave and be branded a traitor in the eyes of those still in authority in the capital, much less face the risk of passing through the roadblocks. Others were desperate to get out and had to be left behind until a spot could be found for them on another convoy.

"We have to hurry," Demers said. "I want to get there before the soldiers and militia at the roadblocks are drunk."

Quickly, they dropped the rear gates of the trucks and began helping people into the backs. The people murmured quietly amongst themselves as they climbed in, helping old people and small children. There were some emotional good-byes, as some of those leaving hugged family and friends who would be staying behind. Then the trucks' back gates were swung up and clanged shut. They were off.

Demers led the little convoy off towards the northeast, heading for safe territory on the far side of the front lines. The rebels were getting closer and closer to the capital, but as they did, government forces and militias became jumpier and more reckless.

Gendarmes manned the first roadblock, but a mass of restless looking Interahamwe militiamen also hung around in the background. They glared venomously, but let the convoy through without incident. The vehicles wound their way through the city's outskirts and towards their destination in the hot afternoon sun.

A few hours later they made it over the lines to the drop-off point and delivered their passengers, a mixture of Tutsis and Hutu moderates. They had managed to save 250 more.

But as Captain Demers later learned, that night the militia finally came into the church. Bursting into the compound, brushing the nuns aside, a few government soldiers appeared, followed by thoroughly drunken and wild-eyed militiamen. Astonishingly, horribly, they singled out children, dragging out into the street over 40 who were under the age of 13. Over the screaming and wailing of the terrified people, they hacked the children to death with machetes on the roadway right in front of the church, leaving the others to clean up the mess. Demers never did find out why they had done that or why they had chosen children, except perhaps to show that they could, and to terrify people.

The June 13 convoy was to be the last refugee movement Demers was able to make from Ste Famille. When he tried to return the next day, militia blocked all access to the site.

Perhaps, too, it was a sign of the increasingly frantic rampage of the extremists as the RPF closed in on the city. Driven on by the desperation of what they knew was happening to their countrymen and relatives in the genocide, the rebel advance proved unstoppable, and by early July they had captured all of Kigali. The extremists fell back in disorder, running wild as they went, looting and killing. Few were killed in the actual fighting of the civil war itself. Most were slaughtered by militiamen, many hacked to death by machetes as groups of militia went from house to house looking for Tutsis (or anyone else they disapproved of) and murdering them right there, or at checkpoints on the roads as the people tried to flee. Bodies sprawled everywhere, creating the horrible stench that all those who were there remember so clearly.

It truly was one of great genocides of the twentieth century. The Nazis' holocaust took six years to kill some six million. In less than three months, the Hutu extremists of Rwanda managed to kill almost 800,000 people, a monthly rate nearly three times higher than that of the Nazis. Even more horrific is the fact that the six million killed by the Nazis came from a population total of almost 100 million, making it approximately one out of sixteen killed in the Holocaust. The 800,000 killed by the Hutu extremists in Rwanda came from a population of less than eight million, making the murder rate in that genocide one out of ten. And this was accomplished not with trains to death camps equipped with gas chambers, but primarily by hand, with bloody machetes.

Even today this terrible dark event haunts most of the Canadians who served there. But the good deeds they managed should not be overshadowed, even by such a horrific event. All Canadians can be proud of what, in the face of such evil, they managed to achieve.

Epilogue
The Great Peace Missions of the 1990s

While the Canadian Forces are still heavily committed abroad today, and the new age of terrorism has brought its own challenges, the years of 1992 to 1995 were the great era of expeditionary peace missions. In 1993 Canada had five formed units simultaneously deployed overseas on peace support missions: three in the Balkans, one in Somalia, and one still in Cyprus. On top of that were the missions, such as UNAMIR in Rwanda, to which Canada contributed personnel as individuals.

And this era of intense peacekeeping burst upon the Canadian Forces suddenly and unexpectedly. As it is so commonly said, Canada virtually invented peacekeeping, starting with the mission to the Sinai to separate the Israelis and Egyptians, for which Lester Pearson won the Nobel Peace Prize in 1957. Throughout the 1960s, 70s, and 80s, Canada contributed to most UN peacekeeping missions, but with the

exception of the 25-year-long commitment of a battalion to
Cyprus, the contingents of that era were either small or short-
lived. Inventors of peacekeeping Canadians may have been,
but throughout those decades, the focus of the Canadian
military was firmly on the central front in Europe. The long
Cold War was an era of garrison training and exercises for a
world war with the U.S.S.R. that thankfully never came.

All of that changed with a bang at the end of the Cold
War. The "new world order" unleashed a rash of ethnic conflicts and instabilities. And finally freed from the straight
jacket of super power standoff, the UN boldly embarked
upon an era of aggressive and widespread peacekeeping
operations. Many were optimistic that the UN would finally
become what it had originally been intended to be — the
world's policeman.

The results, it has to be admitted, were somewhat
mixed. Enthusiasm for UN peacekeeping has abated since
then. But in those three years between 1992 and 1995, the
men and women of the Canadian forces found themselves
awoken from the long slumbers of peacetime soldiering and
thrown headlong into the world's worst trouble spots. The
result was a flurry of improvisation and a whole generation of
often-heroic action in the midst of some of the worst ethnic
conflicts of modern times.

In those circumstances, the Canadian military displayed some remarkable performances. Overstretched and
underequipped, often thrown into untenable circumstances

with unworkable mandates and scant support from the international community, Canada's soldiers improvised, adapted, and overcame. The dramatic stories from that time should make all Canadians proud, and deserve to be told. We live among heroes.

Further Reading

Barnett, Michael. *Eyewitness to a Genocide: The United Nations and Rwanda*. Ithaca, NY: Cornell University Press, 2002.

Dallaire, Roméo. *Shake Hands With the Devil: The Failure of Humanity in Rwanda*. Toronto: Random House Canada, 2003.

MacKenzie, Lewis. *Peacekeeper: The Road To Sarajevo*. Vancouver: Douglas & McIntyre, 1993.

McQuarrie, John. *Between the Lines: Canadians in the Service of Peace*. Toronto: Macmillan Canada, 1993.

Off, Carol. *The Ghosts of Medak Pocket: The Story of Canada's Secret War*. Toronto: Random House Canada, 2004.

Pupetz, Ron (editor). *In the Line of Duty*. Ottawa: Department of National Defence, 1994.

Acknowledgments

As an historian, I had the rare and very fortunate pleasure to have received these amazing stories first hand from the individuals who were profiled and the people that worked with them. They all gave generously of their time and their knowledge and went well beyond what I could have ever hoped for. It was a true honour working with each and every one of them.

The author is indebted to the following people:

Lieutenant General (retired) the Honourable Roméo A. Dallaire — Sir, you are my personal hero and you inspire me daily with your humanity. Thank you for everything you have done and God bless.

Brigadier General Michel Jones, Colonel Jim Calvin, Lieutenant Colonels Jeremy Mansfield, Gord Zans, Simon Hetherington, Majors Brent Beardsley, Don McNeil, Jean-Yves St-Denis, Luc Racine, Andre Demers, and Steve Murray, Captain Dave Murault, Lieutenant Roy Van de Berg, Sergeant Mario Charette, Dr. Pat Haugh, and Mr. Tony LaBoisseirre — thank you for sharing your collective stories. My only hope is that I do justice to all the individuals and their units.

And … David Hyman — you were always on the other end of my email offering whatever assistance you could. Thank you for your patience and for always having an answer.

To our friends and family including Dennis and Brenna

Acknowlegments

Thornton and family, Brigadier General Paul and Mrs. McCabe, my Enslev family, and my Johnston family — thank you. Thanks also to Andrew Chaplin, Charani, Eve Lee, Donna Bain, Jane Barnett, Janice Mitchell, Dale and Lori Summers, and my old high school "Model UN" coach, Mr. Keith Cowell — thank you all, for your proofreading and your comments. Even your criticisms were supportive! Thank you also to Kara Turner, my editor at Altitude Publishing for her advice and for giving me the chance to tell these fantastic and amazing stories.

And lastly, to my husband and children. Thank you for bringing out the inner walrus in me and for letting me hog the computer with the internet, phone, and study space. Thank you for putting up with The Jam at full volume as part of my creative process. Thank you for allowing me to read chapter bits to you instead of your night-time bed stories and for decorating all my interview notes with glitter and SpongeBob stickers. This book was written with love for you so that you can always know that heroes really do walk amongst us. We must never forget those who need our help and never forget that it is an honour to do one's duty.

About the Author

Sheila Enslev Johnston is a proud military brat who has lived around the world with her military father, Jens Enslev. Generation after generation of the Enslev family has served as soldiers, both in Canada and in Denmark. Sheila continued this tradition by joining the Canadian Armed Forces in 1986. First classified as a communications officer, she transferred to the artillery when the Armed Forces opened up the combat arms to women, making her one of Canada's first female artillery officers.

Sheila left the army to continue her academic studies in military affairs, but has remained passionate in her support of the Canadian Armed Forces. She has worked as a defence analyst for the Conference of Defence Associations and provided geo-political and military research to Jane's Defence of Great Britain. She has published numerous academic papers within her field, but her most personal project to date was her children's book, *A Father to Be Proud Of*. This brightly coloured picture book explains a father's absence to his young children as he prepares to leave on a United Nations tour. Being raised by a single father within the military culture, Sheila is deeply committed to all issues of quality of life and family support. She has served on various Military Family Resource Centre (MFRC) boards of directors and sat for four years on the National Advisory Board for Military Families.

Sheila is married to Major Paul Johnston and has four children; Kelcei, Jens, McCauseland, and Samuel. She dreams of doing field work with the United Nations when her young family has grown older but for now, Sheila has been concentrating upon her writing career and trying to balance research with soccer practices.

Photo Credits

Cover: CP PHOTO/Tom Hanson; Colonel Jim Calvin: page 41; Mario Charette: page 81; Couvrette Studios: page 10; Steven Murray: page 46.

Amazing Author
Question and Answer

What was your inspiration for writing about this topic?

I am a strong supporter of the United Nations and, in particular, peacekeeping. Peacekeeping is a very proud part of our Canadian heritage, and I believe the United Nations is a crucial international organization. I have had the opportunity to work with the UN in a theatre of operations, and have been thoroughly impressed with their dedication and professionalism as they work towards a world of peace.

What surprised you most while you were researching the topic?

What surprised me most was discovering how many incredible stories of courage and heroism there are, that have never been told to the Canadian public. As Canadians, we can be very proud of our peacekeepers.

Which person or people do you most admire in this Amazing Story?

It will come as no surprise to anyone that Lieutenant General Roméo Dallaire remains my personal hero. His heart is enormous, and his compassion for others is beyond admirable. Additionally, all the people I talked to were "men among men" (and women, too, of course!). They leave their families and their comfortable homes in order to serve six-month tours of duty in war-torn hellholes around the world. They do this because they believe in the sanctity of human life, and believe peace is worth striving for. To me, these soldiers, sailors, and air force personnel are the true heroes in our society. They are paid little, yet they bring our country great honour.

What escapade did you most identify with?

I probably identified most with Lieutenant Colonel Jones and his Van Doos, when they had difficulty with the Serbian checkpoint guards. I had a similar experience when I was in Croatia, made worse by the fact that I was a young female. The guards that made my passage difficult were Croatian militia, rather than Serbian, but it was an equally tense, very scary situation for me at the time. The professionalism of the driver I was with, however, smoothed our passage through the crossing.

What difficulties did you run into when researching this topic?

My research presented few difficulties. Everyone I approached — from the Department of National Defence to individual soldiers — fell over themselves to be helpful. Any difficulties

I did have were of my own making, in the sense that telling these stories was accompanied by an incredible sense of responsibility to make sure they were told right — told with absolute accuracy. I wanted to honour the individuals I wrote about, and to do them justice.

Why did you become a writer? Who inspired you?

I have been writing since I was a young child — doing research, at the age of seven, about the 100 Years' War! I have always found it easier to write my thoughts than to articulate them. Another reason I write is because my family, like many military families, has moved all over the world, and writing allows me to stay connected with Canada and to do the work I love, no matter where we are posted. It also allows me to be accessible to my children and my husband. I can make my own schedule, and make sure I don't miss Christmas concerts or soccer games.

What part of the writing process did you enjoy most?

Definitely, it was talking to the individuals involved and hearing their stories. Everyone I interviewed was just incredible, and I am immensely honoured to have met them all.

What is your next project?

I have just started writing another book (again, for Altitude Publishing) about the Afghanistan war.

Who are your Canadian heroes?

Again, I have been very outspoken over the years in my admiration of Lieutenant General Roméo Dallaire, and not necessarily for the reasons that some might think. Yes, he showed incredible heroism while in Rwanda, but his actions since coming home are also very heroic. He has been instrumental in improving the quality of life for military families, and has been an outspoken advocate for soldiers suffering from post-traumatic stress disorder (PTSD). Dallaire made it okay for soldiers to admit that sometimes these United Nations tours take incredible tolls on both the individual and the family. He has also started a non-profit charity to help support children affected by war (for more information, go to www. roméodallaire.com), and he personally funds Rwandan orphans in their schooling. He is a great man, and I feel so honoured to know him.

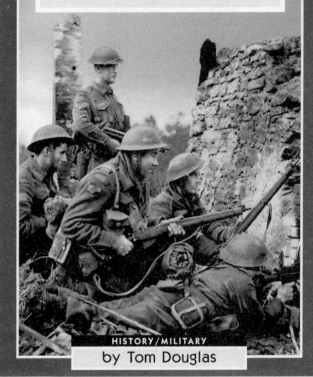

GREAT CANADIAN WAR HEROES
Victoria Cross Recipients
of World War II

"As I watched him lead his men through that thundering barrage, I felt a quiver run up and down my spine. I'd never seen anything like it."
War correspondent Wallace Reyburn

Of all the decorations a combatant in the Commonwealth can receive, none is more prestigious than the Victoria Cross. This book tells the inspiring stories of the 16 Canadians who received the Victoria Cross during World War II. These men came from all walks of life and from various ranks within the Canadian Forces, but they all had one thing in common: each displayed exceptional bravery and self-sacrifice in the face of danger.

 True stories. Truly Canadian.

ISBN 1-55439-057-5

OTHER AMAZING STORIES

These titles are available wherever you buy books. If you have trouble finding the book you want, call the Altitude order desk at **1-800-957-6888**, e-mail your request to: **orderdesk@altitudepublishing.com** or visit our Web site at **www.amazingstories.ca**

New **AMAZING STORIES** titles are published every month.